PILLARS OF INDUSTRIAL DEMOCRACY

- ❖ HUMAN RELATIONS
- ❖ EMPLOYEES PARTICIPATION
- ❖ EMPLOYEES INVOLVEMENT
- ❖ EMPLOYEES EMPOWERMENT

Authored By

DR. VR KATKHEDE

notionpress.com

INDIA • SINGAPORE • MALAYSIA

Notion Press

Old No. 38, New No. 6
McNichols Road, Chetpet
Chennai - 600 031

First Published by Notion Press 2018
Copyright © VR Katkhede 2018
All Rights Reserved.

ISBN 978-1-64249-470-9

CONTENTS

PREFACE

If you don't know where you are going, then you will not take the right road which will take you there. The same thing happens there with organization. Without vision, resources are underutilized, organizational purpose is unfulfilled and individual energy and momentum are misdirected. Therefore, shared vision is critical for organizational success. A clear vision liberates energy, promotes alignment and focus and ensures proactive and productive action. A shared vision allows individuals and organizations to extend less energy and to maximize output. A clear vision aligns people, passion, resources and energy in the appropriate direction thereby creating your organization's future. This will take you and your people through the processes of participation, involvement and empowerment to create a shared vision for themselves, their department and the organization as a whole. It will help them to identify the appropriate strategies and actions on the part of leader and his people that are needed to make their vision a reality.

Surviving and certainly thriving in today's environment will require new levels of organizational agility and innovation. These in turn, will require people with autonomy who can respond quickly, intelligently, creatively and purposefully in the best interest of the whole organization aligning with each other and acting in unison. Self organizing systems require people who understand the business – its core ideology, its goals and strategy, its competitive position and business situation and its volume. They also need people who can address novel situations with disciplined thinking and can through the use of disciplined interaction processes, join with others act in unified way.

Employee empowering organizations have developed social infrastructures, processes, systems and structures that enabled them to act in a unified way to strengthen their creative potential, improve its competitive position and reach its vision of the ideal – excellence. Their processes are designed to maximize the capability, will and energy of people. The systems are designed to be simple, flexible, allowing for key variables, which in long run will lead to highly visible revenues. Further, these structures are designed to minimize the level of wasteful resources to provide flexibility, integrative decision making and self accountability. This has been achieved through local employee autonomy, participation and empowerment of employees without any dispersion of efforts. They have done it by participating, involving and then empowering employees. Every part of an individuals in these organizations are aligned toward some comprehensive set of governing ideas including vision, benefits, values principles, goals and strategies for achieving alignment and unified action, from the perspective of organization and its people. What emerges from the PIE operation is what is called 'life giving forces' such as; sense of ownership, partnership, freedom of expression, trust, respect, and risk taking.

An organization is a place where we get our work done. How well we perform in our work areas is dependent on the following observations made by various highly empowered organizations around the world.

- ❖ Work processes are organized to produce results.
- ❖ Workplaces are organized to enable employees to perform their tasks.
- ❖ Employee relations are organized and coordinated to enable coordinated actions.
- ❖ Competence of an employee corresponds with tasks.
- ❖ Competence of an employee is adopted and integrated in the work process.

- ❖ Competence of an employee is engaged and released in the performance of work.
- ❖ Competence is coordinated in collaborative and cooperative actions at work.
- ❖ Engagement and involvement of an employee in the workplace occurs through personal responsibility, autonomy and self-management.
- ❖ The ability to be responsible is an integral choices and so is in accepting consequences of his action.
- ❖ A participatory strategy in the is incorporated with engagement and involvement of the people.

These values are supported by the belief that all human beings are able to function and act responsibly as long as their working conditions are organized in a way that allow them to do so. Self management and self leadership, it is seen provide considerable promise for taking the pursuit for employers effectiveness to the next level. Indeed effectively self-led employees, both behaviourally and cognitively, offer the best results for achieving employee and organizational effectiveness.

When an employee works responsibly and independently at work based on personal freedom and mutual trust, he achieves the level of modus operandi in taking charge of himself in the workplace. At this point there will no longer be a need for anyone in the workplace to give handouts. Independence through responsible choices and actions ensures the effectiveness of a job; hence, the practice of taking control in a significant way stimulates and inspires self-esteem and self-confidence which showcases the art and skill of a responsible person. Such an application of participatory strategy, as a way to optimize the outcomes of work processes, work performances and collaborative activities, lead to the implementation of a democratic form of work organization. This form of work organization is designed in a way that is congruous with the values of human beings and therefore such organizations should comply with the following requirements:

- ❖ The employees in the organization participate directly in decision making processes concerning their own work.
- ❖ Participation and involvement by the employees means that they have authority to make autonomous decisions within their respective field of work.
- ❖ Empowerment means that employees have the authority to influence decision-making that will positively enhance their effectiveness in their work fields.

The organizational form that complies with these characteristics is a 'model democratic workplace' that combines the elements of industrial democracy, and therefore, we must take into consideration the consequences and effects of such form in connection with the structure and processes at workplace. The objective of giving authority to the employees must support the principle of rule by the people and therefore the concomitant governance practices must necessarily reflect this principle of this organizational structure, its culture, its processes, its leadership, its style and its policies; such a participatory style is called Industrial Democracy. It is also to be noted that Industrial Democracy has two elements: inner and outer democracy. While inner democracy grants everyone at work an adequate measure personal authority to perform their jobs as responsible persons - which is the source of participatory democracy - outer democracy, on the other hand, is based on the belief of governance by external authorities which regulate this authority through legislations, policies, practices and specific contracts. The collective bargaining and appointment of a worker director on the governing board is the best example of an outer democracy. However, for all this to happen, the assurance of the employee's participation and involvement in their respective fields of work is mandatory and necessarily constitutes the main pillars on which the foundation of industrial democracy is built upon.

Finally, we can conclude that participatory management style as a positive trend and not a threat to authority. As the saying goes, "the more managers count on controlling, the more out of control things become; the more managers share their power, the more powerful they become."

In conclusion, industrial democracy is a new intervention that projects a distributed form of leadership, thereby changing the role of the traditional leader from one of command and rigidity to that of sharing and positive influencing. This will result in the promotion of a common organizational mission: passion for excellence and the conduct of business that would excite their employees. It would mean that in the framework of industrial democracy, employees will work to ensure that they can contribute significantly to the organization's mission, goals and objectives.

This is the message that is conveyed throughout this book to all organizational leaders, managers, employees, management students and readers in general.

– **Dr. VR Katkhede**

Chapter 1

INTRODUCTION

A. Values of the Human Element; Humanistic, Optimistic and Democratic

B. PIE – Some Implications and Assumptions

C. PIE and Democratic Workplace

"Industrial democracy is not about everyone voting
but everyone have a vote"

Chapter 1
INTRODUCTION

Before turning to the issues as to how employee participation, involvement and empowerment is being practiced through the ages; let us look at some actual. It is conclusively cleared that no act of human being in any social Endeavour is completed without cooperation and coordination of each other. Weather it is stated, unstated implied or applied, do need carrying out management activities in the organization. Although, sometimes we believe that it is a myth but it is reality of working life. No management can carry out production activities or earn profit without the participation of employees.

"People acting together as a group can accomplish things, which no individual acting alone could ever hope to bring about."

– (Franklin D. Roosevelt)

In this context, it can be rightly said as; "coming together is a beginning, moving together is a progress and working together is a success." The only successful mantra for this is employee participation, involvement and empowerment in their work activities.

YOU CAN BUILD HUMAN RELATIONS ONLY IF YOU ARE IN TOUCH WITH THE PEOPLE

– Dr. VR Katkhede

INTRODUCTION

Every firm has an organizational behavior system. It includes the organization's stated or unstated philosophy, values, vision, mission and goals, the quality of leadership, communication and group dynamics, the nature of both formal and informal organization, influence of the social environment. These issues combined together, create a culture in the organization, where in personal attitudes of employees and situational factors can produce motivation and goal achievement. While reviewing the history of organization's renewal, we have witnessed autocratic custodial, supportive, collegial systems fit organizations. It is also seen the supportive, collegial and system models are more consistent with contemporary employee's needs and therefore will predictably obtain more effective results in many situations. Management must examine the management style they are using, determine weather it is most appropriate one and remain flexible in their use of alternative and emerging models.

In collaborative management one of the important things is to manage in organizations is culture. The prevailing patterns of values, beliefs, attitudes, assumptions, expectations, activities, interactions, norms, and sentiments. Secondly, managing culture should be collaborative business of widespread participation in creating and managing a culture that satisfies the wants and needs of individuals and at the same time that it fosters the organization's purposes. Collaborative management of the culture means that everyone not just a small group has stake in making the organization work. Just as visioning, empowerment, learning problem solving processes are opportunities for collaboration in the organization; so is the managing culture. Culture is the bedrock of behavior in any organization. The reciprocal influence among culture strategy structure style and processes makes each important and each influences the others. So culture consist basic assumptions, values, behavior, that are viewed as the correct way to perceive, think and feel. That is why cultural change is necessary for the true organizational improvement. The definition also places considerable weight on organizational processes: and processes are how to get things done. Processes are relatively easy to change, but change becomes permanent.

When the culture change and people accept the new way as the right way. We believe that when the culture promotes collaboration, empowerment, participation and involvement and continuous learning, the organization is bound to succeed.

A. VALUES; HUMANISTIC; OPTIMISTIC AND DEMOCRATIC

A set of historical values, assumptions and beliefs supported by research studies or various social thinkers,' reformers constitutes an integral part of employee's participation, improvement in management affair. Most of the beliefs were formulated early in the development of the given field and they continue to evolve as the field itself evolves. These values and assumptions are developed from research and theory by behavioral scientists and from experiences and observations of practicing managers and organizational leaders. These assumptions and beliefs that are so valuable and obviously correct that they are taken for granted and are rarely examined or questioned. These values, assumptions and beliefs provide structure and stability for people as they attempt to understand the world around them. Participation, involvement, empowerment, values and beliefs tend to be humanistic, optimistic and democratic.

Humanistic values proclaim the importance of the individual: it respects the whole person, treat people with respect and dignity, it assumes that everyone has humanistic worth, view all people as having the potential for growth and development. Optimistic values posit that people are basically good, that progress is possible and desirable in human affairs and that rationality, reason and goodwill are the tools for making progress. Democratic values assert the sanctity of the individual, the right of people to be free from arbitrary misuse of power and authority, the importance of fair and equitable treatment to all and the need for justice through the rule of law and due process. Evidences for the validity of these values and their supporting assumptions comes from many historical sources – Hawthrone studies, the human relations movement, the clash between labor and capital, increasing awareness of the dysfunctions of bureaucracy,

Taylorism practices, effect of the different leadership styles, greater understanding of individual motivation and team and team working group dynamics and the like. Values and assumption do not spring full grown from individuals or societies. They are formed from the collective beliefs or the spirit of the time. All these ingredients accumulated, they were the foundation for the theory and practice of employee participation, involvement and empowerment.

THE CHRONOLOGY CAPTURE

(see chapter II)

Most of the significant influences from research theory and observations and experiences utilized by industrial people, organizational practitioners, and academicians to summarise the intellectual climate of this period. The initial enthusiasm for scientific management and bureaucracy gave way to authoritarian leadership because of increasing doubt as theory and research pointed out their limitations, dysfunctions and negative consequences. In response, democratic-thinking employers and entrepreneurs formulated a set of values and assumptions regarding people, groups and organizations that were, as we have said, humanistic, optimistic and democratic. It is our belief that most democratic thinkers and practitioners held humanistic and democratic values with implications for different and better way to run organizations and to deal with people in different situations. The democratic values prompted a critique of authoritarian, autocratic and arbitrary management practices as well as pointing out the dysfunctions of bureaucracies. The humanistic values promoted a search for better ways to run organizations and develop the people in them.

B. PARTICIPATION, INVOLVEMENT AND EMPOWERMENT

Some Implications and Assumptions

Two basic assumptions about individuals, groups and organizations persuade democratic workplace. First assumption is that most individuals most individuals are driven toward personal growth and development, if provided an environment that is both supportive and changing, since, by nature, people are driven to develop their inherent potential. The second basic and natural assumption conveys the fact that most people desire to make a significant contribution to attaining the goals of an organization within the given parameters. With a basic understanding of inherent human potential and the concomitant desire of people to make and acquire a sense of satisfactory contribution to their profession, the organization can greatly facilitate a substantial amount of constructive energy from their employees. Further, it has been observed that experienced people in their respective professions are generally experts after a given time and therefore they, but naturally, are desirous of upgrading their skills through creativity – that is researching better and more effective ways of the doing the work in a shorter time. The implications of these two assumptions are very straight forward and the management therefore needs to focus on such pointers as: asking, listening, supporting, challenging, encouraging, encouraging risk-taking, permitting human failure, removing obstacles and barriers, giving autonomy and responsibilities, setting high standard and rewarding successes. Finally the assumption is that many attitudinal and motivational problems in organizations require interactive and transactional solutions, such problems have greatest chance of constructive solution if all parties in the system alter their mutual relationships. A key assumption in industrial democracy is that the needs and aspirations of human beings are the reason for organized efforts in society. This belief suggests strongly that it is good to acquire a sense of developmental outlook and to seek opportunities where people can experience personal and professional growth. Such an orientation creates a self-fulfilling prophecy in the belief that people are important tends to result in the actuality of their being important. The principles of industrial democracy believe that people can grow, develop and enhance their competency through optimistic developmental attitudes. Acquiring such a set of assumptions about people is most likely to reap rewards which would most certainly be beneficial to both, organizations and their employees.

It is possible to create organizations on the one hand and humane developmental and empowering on other hand, which will prove to be high performing in terms of productivity, quality, profitability. Evidence for this assumptions come from numerous examples where, "putting people first" paid off handsomely in profit and performance. The implication is that people are organizations most important resources, they are the source of productivity and profit and should be treated with care. An organization's competitive advantage stems from people and people produce those results depending on the way that they are treated and managed. This is the reason why top performing companies command a superior all-round position as compared to mediocre companies as they are better organized to meet the needs of their employees than their competitors. Resultantly, employees of such organizations are greatly motivated to do a superior job in whatever are their areas of specialization. This also means that these employees are better organized and therefore adequately prepared to meet the needs of their customers in terms total customer satisfaction, economy of services, punctuality as well as in anticipating their customers' future needs. The friendly and motivating culture of an organization most certainly allows its employees to voluntarily participate and involve themselves in the company's all-round progress; this also offers the employees the vital opportunity of empowering themselves in their work places, their organizations and in relationship to their management and customers. From the management's point of view, a good and reciprocal climate allows employees to achieve their desired future and to create their workplaces that have meaning and community. This will enable the management to use structural interventations for creating democratic workplaces, as well as the implementation of certain socio-technical systems to jointly optimize. Further, the implementations of such systems as Management by Objectives (MBO), Quality of Worklife (QWL), Total Quality Management (TQM), along with organizational restructuring, and renewal-transformations. Through all such interventions employee participation, involvement and empowerment (PIE) this is considered the key to getting people to want to participate in positive change in high performing organizations.

High performing democratic workplaces have some values developed of their own. In a nutshell, transforming organizations from command-and-control way of operating to a more democratic style, results in the following:

- ❖ Increase in productivity, profitability and efficiency
- ❖ Increase ability to attract top talent and decrease in voluntary turnover.
- ❖ Increase in employee engagement.
- ❖ Increase in level of creativity and innovation.
- ❖ Increase in organizational alignment and overall level of trust.
- ❖ Increase in an organization's overall adaptability and agility.
- ❖ A heightened level of civic engagement by employee in the organization's community.
- ❖ Greater say in day-to-day management issues.

Such democratic workplaces provide values because it is comprehensive and systematically transforms an organization's environment and culture while developing leaders at every level throughout the organizations.

C. PIE AND DEMOCRATIC WORKPLACE

The field of industrial democracy rests on the foundation of values and assumptions about people and organizations. This belief helps to define what employee involvement and empowerment is. Employee participation and involvement is then not something that the management does to the employee but rather helps to create a mindset for the employees in regard to their roles in the organization. The management can then create a context that allows for the empowering of the organization's employees so that they see themselves as possessors of freedom, confidence and discretion in their work professions; this will impart to them a sense of personal commitment to their employers and their organization as a whole. James Belasco emphasizes this very vividly in his book, "Teaching Elephants To Dance". His book enumerates the following pointers:

- ❖ Only massive changes will suffice to keep organization viable in the future.
- ❖ People will not naturally embrace the needed changes.
- ❖ Empowerment is the key to getting people to want to participate in change.

Developing a clear vision, devising a strategy to achieve the vision and unleashing the intelligence and energy of the workforce to accomplish the vision are what empowerment is all about. According to Belasco, involvement and participation energize greater performance, produce better solutions to the problems and greatly enhance acceptance of decisions. To empower is to give someone power, which is done by giving individuals the authority, to make decisions, to contribute to their ideas, to experts influence and to be responsible, participation is an especially effective form of employment participation, enhances empowerment and empowerment in turn enhances performance and individuals well being and ultimately democratic values of doing the things.

It is becoming increasingly clear that the engine of organizational development is not the business of analysts but, on the contrary, that of managers and their employees. A work system that functions without the altering human knowledge, skills, behaviors and attitude changes in the technology processes, structures and practices is unlikely to yield long term benefits. Managing business productivity has essentially became synonymous with meaningful and effective changes. To manage change, companies must not only determine what to do and how to do it, but they also need to concern themselves as to how their employees will react to the change. In this respect, the role of Human Resource Management (HRM) is moving from traditional command and control approach to a more strategic one based on the principles of industrial democracy.

Employee Participation, Involvement and Empowerment (PIE) are the milestones of the path of evolution towards collaborative management. The very survival of organizations depend on their ability to move from present traditional philosophy to such collaborative philosophy. PIE is beyond bureaucracy challenge. People-oriented organizations are genuinely fit for the use of human beings by extending to them a free and inspiring work environment which are in nature progressive and democratic. These are the organizations which create inspiring and engaging work atmospheres for their employees. This makes every employee to align with a deep sense of purpose in which management assumptions and practices inspire and unleash imagination, creativity, initiative and energy from all corners of the organizations. They adopt proactive people-management practices with a more agile management system thereby replacing a rigid hierarchy. This occasions a vibrant social systems for the organization which is very important to an organization's commitment to OD and change management. Empowered employees lead to positive results for employees, their manager and their organizations. Business leaders and the HR professionals have generally agreed that empowered employees exhibit a high degree of commitment, productivity and loyalty to their work and workplace. However, for the good of the organization and individuals, consultative, collaborative and cooperative help may sometimes call for confrontation, questioning and challenging to given organizational situations but this would ultimately transform the stage from one of conflict to that of cooperation. Historically, the PIE system had to go through time-consuming processes to result in today's democracy at the workplace.

Most of the literature reviewed on PIE centers on psychological and social empowerment measured by collective efficacy – the belief that people together can make a difference. Outcome efficacy – the belief that one's action can produce results. Political efficacy – the belief that one can influence the political process, communities in organizations and critical thinking ability and participatory behavior. Psychological and social empowerment significantly associated with increased participation.

PIE is culture and people specific that requires actions within the organizational context. PIE cannot be seen as a stand-alone strategy, but it is part of comprehensive approach engaging organizational leaders to promote structural, social, cultural and policy changes to support employee engagement.PIE strategies, therefore, mean challenging control and in justice through social and cultural processes, and in doing so, it uncovers the organization's control levers of traditional barriers. This enables employees to challenge internalized oppression and to develop new representations of reality. PIE can be seen as a dynamic interplay between gaining better internal control or capacity – personal transformation and overcoming external barriers to accessing resources. In short, PIE influences employees ability to get through collective participation by strengthening their organizational capacities, challenging power, inequities and achieving outcomes on many reciprocal levels in different domains–psychological, social, employee relations and engagement, enhanced cohesion, togetherness greater access to organizational resources, open governance and transformed organization.

In today's changing organizations, managing employees is not a matter of manipulation. It is about working with your employees on a partnership basis to achieve strategic goals of the organization. It is therefore, management's duty to study the character, the nature and performance of it's workforce with a view to finding out their limitations on one hand but even more important, their possibilities for development on the other hand, and then systematically to train, help, teach, involve and participate them wherever it is possible, those opportunities for advancement which will finally enable them to do highest and most interesting work for which their natural abilities fit them in the organization in which they are employed.

Ultimately, the question will be as to how management leaders will manage their employees in practice and this will depend on what assumptions they make about their employees. There are times when management leaders simply assume, without any legitimate evidence, that their employees habitually procrastinate in their work or irresponsibly avoid doing their work, and so the management treats them as such – this attitude on the part of the management actually causes the employees to behave in this manner. On the other hand, if management leaders assume that employees welcome challenges, involvement, participation, contribution, etc., then they would respond accordingly. P. Drucker has rightly observed that "management is not a mere discipline but a culture with its own values, beliefs, tools and language." If employees are allowed to participate respectfully, unbiasedly, conscientioualy and independently, they will then involve themselves willingly in work activities and will surely achieve their goals with better and more satisfactory results. Therefore, management cannot and should not apply one set of assumption to fit all situations.

In today's knowledge era it is imperative for the management to create a thriving work environment to facilitate the creation, sharing, using and reusing of employees knowledge which obviously demands management to focus employees PIE. When an employee sees high productivity and workplace improvements as a path to the attainment of one or more of his personal goals, he will tend to be a high producer. The twentieth century was the age of machine, the twenty-first century will be the age of people. Employees with high involvement and participation are empowered employees, they are satisfied employees and therefore more productive. Managing people today is about giving the opportunity to people to develop and to make contribution to organization. Employees can be energized, engaged and involved in problem solving and mobilized for change in participative structure that permits them to venture beyond their normal work roles to take meaningful organizational issues. This is possible only through collaborative and tolerant culture that enables employees to recreate themselves. Highly empowered organizations where employees continuously expanding their capacity to create results they truly desire, where new thinking is nurtured and where collective aspirations are set free. Their emphasis is on employees in organization wanting to learn and wanting to develop their talent facilitated in such organizational culture.

In this book, we have attempted to present a concise but complete exposition of PIE practices in the belief that readers, organization leaders, management executives, management students, academicians and practitioners and consultants can use this book to know, implement it in their institutions for the betterment of human side of an enterprise. I hope, it will help and guide them a lot for finding out suitable solutions to positive and proactive man-management practices.

Chapter 2
HUMAN RELATIONS THROUGH AGES

A. Historical Review of Literature

- Agricultural Revolution – Slave Management System
- Free Artisan System
- Guild System
- Paternalistic Management System
- Factory System
- Labor Movement – Rise of Trade Unions
- Labor Welfare System
- Scientific Management
- Human Relations Movement
- Behavioral Sciences Contribution

B. Human Relations – Historical Studies

- Mary Parkor Follet
- C.I., Barnar
- Lewin And Whyte
- The Hawthrone Studies
- Lester Cocn
- Carl Regars
- Burn And Stalkas
- R. Likert

Chapter 2
HUMAN RELATIONS THROUGH AGES

Several revolutionary changes occurred in the industrial field in the 20ᵗʰ century and continue to occur in 21ˢᵗ century. The changes have been significant. Public – opinion has forced management and labor alike to adopt reasonable approaches to their problems in tune with the changing industrial and social scene. Both have learned to recognize the social, moral and organizational responsibilities. Events have encouraged mature, long range responsible thinking on both the sides and a desire to work together at work……

HUMAN RELATIONS THROUGH AGES – HISTORICAL REVIEW

Several revolutionary changes occurred in the industrial field in the 20ᵗʰ century. These changes have not only affected the methods and techniques of production but changes have been also witnessed in human relations era. The commodity concept of employee has been changed to participative concept of employee. Various researchers, thinkers, social reformers and industrialist have advocated, through their research, experience and observations that an employee is a co-partner in industry. Thus, the industrial democratic atmosphere started emerging gradually in which the employees and the management are involved in decision- making processes. Decision-making is not only the concern of management alone, but equally that of the employees so that a joint responsibility is exercised regarding commonality of matters between the management and the employees. Given that the main objective of any commercial enterprise is profit maximization, nevertheless, it is important to note that the reaping of higher profits is the result of the co-operation extended by the employees to the management. Therefore, if employees are allowed to participate in decision-making processes, they will certainly feel that they have had a say in decision-making as well as having acquired a better understanding of industrial processes of which they are the part of. Organizational changes from slavery to democracy in the work place is closely related with the basic changes in the fabric of society. Changes in social organizations as regards their structure and management have been part and parcel of the transition from the simple and single unit. The small sized industry in which the roles of owner, manager and accountant were managed by one person as compared to today's massive multi-unit complex share-holding organizations, which are divided into specialized departments and geographically shows the extent of this industrial transformation. Changes have been significant. Public opinion has forced management and labor alike to adopt reasonable approaches to their problems in tune with the changing social scene. Both have learned to recognize their social, moral, and organizational responsibilities. Events have encouraged mature, long-range, responsible thinking on both the sides and a desire to work together at work. But track to this change has not been smooth; on the contrary the organization man has travelled a long and hard path with stresses and strains to reach in present position in the organization, enjoying freedom of self-expression. Thus the history of laboring class is largely the history of his legal, social and economic status. His checkered progress has been from the status of a slave or serf, through that of free artisan, guild system and factory to the present self-expression in modern organization. In order to understand the present position of the employee in the organization in a broader perspective, it is thought necessary to trace his journey from agrarian labor to the modern day self-expressed employee.

CHANGING HUMAN RELATIONS – HISTORICAL BACKGROUND

1. Agricultural Revolution

The period characterized by the existence of serf, slaves and few artisans is generally described as an agricultural period where pre-dominant-unit of productions was the manor and the principal product were agricultural. The most common type of employer-employee relationship (in this phase) was that in which employers were masters and employees were essentially slaves. The slave was a chattel, the personal property of his master. Management of slave manpower was provided by the owner who used to utilize rule-of-thumb techniques. The worker, under this system, was just like a commodity; one could cheaply buy him from the market to be exploited. One could hire and fire the slave at will as per the requirement of immediacy of the firm. The working conditions in the production units of this era were brutal and back-breaking, man worked from dawn until dusk under intolerable conditions of diseases, filth, danger and scarcity of resources. He had to work this way to live. Human relations practices were almost lacking but not because they were not needed. The condition of exploitative hard work and poverty were simply not an appropriate environment for development of human relations.

2. Free Artisans

Gradually from the limited specialization of function among slaves and serfs, the status of free artisans developed. With the passing years, increasing number of artisans achieved a status of independence and were thus able to sell their services for wages. Specialization of productive processes increased and independent craftsmen consequently found their economic positions strengthened. They began to form craft guilds.

3. Guild System

The guild slowly found its way both among the merchants and craftsmen. Merchants guild were made up of local distributors who bonded together to set local standard of quality and protect themselves against competition from outside. Within the craft organizations, clear cut differentiation separated master craft man (the entrepreneurs of the system), journeymen (its wage earners) and apprentices. Journeymen and apprentices worked together with the master craft man, generally in the latter's home. The primary obligation of the master was to train the apprentice in the skill of the craft so that he would someday quality as a journeyman or a master. The master had the right to discipline him and in general was responsible for his good conduct, his approach being that of a father to his son. In some cases, he could not even marry without the consent of the masters. In general, the bond between the master and the apprentice was the closest description, the master stood in loco parentis to the apprentice who associated with him in the workshop and at the home in terms of personal intimacy. In this way, the concept of man as a commodity which was cold and impersonal was replaced by the personal and sometimes super personal attitudes of paternalism which made his "boss" the looker after his employees or subordinates.

4. Paternalism

When the business was relatively small and products were simple the top management (leader) tended to adopt without much rationalization a pattern of organization based on patriarchal family. As the business was small, the leader of the businessman knew his help and they knew him. He know whether they worked or loafed and whether they are drunken or sober; usually he gave some attention to the welfare of his own people. He helped them when they were in trouble and remonstrated over derelictions from duty. In fact, he frequently forgave those who owed him some considerations and from whom he might expect in return respectful and pliable behavior. He seems to have accepted some responsibility and made modest efforts to serve the good of all who he saw had benefited from it. Paternalism, however, had its own weaknesses. It did not inspire the worker to do more than the minimum required to keep safer from being fired. The approach inherent in this paternalism was autocratic, treating the workers more as objects. The bestowal of benefits on workers was accompanied by the contempt that the workers are incapable of moral choice. Paternalism is supposed to arrest and annihilate the initiative in the worker. To live on the doles or rewards which are the fruits of compassion hurts the pride of the worker. It is detrimental to his self-respect. The rewards if regularized soon lose their novelty and special purpose. Once an incentive is committed it should not be withdrawn. With the disappearance of paternalism the equation between the worker and the leader underwent a major change – from that of a warm and caring paternal relationship to that of a materialistic relationship where each sought to exploit the other to the best possible extent. Initially, it was considered that the only motivational factor for the worker was his work and the physical condition of the work. Later, with the manager/leader/management being no more the role model of the caretaker or "big daddy" to the worker, the equation between the trusted paternal entrepreur and the worker/apprentice ceased to exist and a new equation of untrustworthiness between worker and manager/management commenced. By the end of the "great depression" period, the concept of loyalty was all but dead.

5. Putting-Out – System

As time moved on, the relationships among the masters of the guild, journeymen and apprentices turned disharmonious. The harmony of the guild system was destroyed by the increasing difficulty for the journeymen and apprentices in attaining the rank of their masters in the realms of production for profit. Gradually these masters got concentrated in their hands production techniques, tools of productions and practices. In this way control of industry was transferred to the trade capitalist. The emergence of the capitalist however, displaced the home production system, and confined both production and worker to the factory. The trade capitalist transformed the craft man into a wage worker and the relations were tied with cash nexus, ultimately contractual in nature. The worker received wages from the entrepreneur and the entrepreneur received the finished product from the workers. In this case, the worker was entirely separated from the means of production and personal ties with such owners were completely lost to the worker. Indeed industrial history cannot ignore this increasing economic power of owners.

6. Factory System – Industrial Revolution

The emergence of industrial proletariat, factory system, and money economy required a kind of worker who was no longer tied with the regulations of craft guild. The factory system required relatively free mobile worker who could sell his labor at will. All these changes occurred due to the industrial revolution, which transformed the work which was so far largely private to a predominantly public one, supporting big enterprises of large scale transformation, merchandise and the like. Secondly, millions of people were forced to spend their entire lives in relative obscurity as farmers. Hunters, pastoralists, or individual craft men were bought together in increasingly large aggregates, where their work behavior was under almost continuous observation and control. Consequently, with the emergence of the industrial revolution, domestic manufacture began to decline thereby causing a migration of the artisans and craftsmen from their villages to the new industrial cities. The rise of factories also led to widespread exploitation of women and child labor. Long hours of labor, low wages and poor working conditions were often intolerable. The ideas of protective legislation was yet unknown. In general, the period was of suffering and hardship for the working classes.

The growing size of the industrial units, the lack of complete absence of personal relations between manager and the worker, administration of rewards and enjoyment deprived from the attachment to work and unhealthy exploitation of the workers have led in such a situation where the conditions of labor were worse than those of the slave. The philosophy of the day, the 19th century, that human happiness was best secured by giving to the capital absolute control over the lives and liberties of man management. Thus the dehumanizing situation in which the worker found himself during these days was aptly brought out in the concept of 'alienation', which meant that the worker become stranger to his own labor over which he lost all power. The worker turned to be a mere 'cog in the machine' and his life one of monotony and boredom.

7. Labor Movement – Rise of Trade Unionism

Civilization has always been built up with the necessity of confirming to the requirement of organized collective life. One cannot bark in the morning sun, sun of the new day without casting a shadow behind. We must not be led astray into painting a picture of the early factory system that is usually dark. No doubt, industrial revolution rendered the rich richer and the poor poorer. But on the whole the factory system brought to the common man more advantages than disadvantages in spite of the industrial revolution having caused social unrest, low wages and disparaging working conditions. Whenever the voice of the movement was suppressed, it emerged into a greater resistance. The discontentment at the economic base coupled with socio-political craving and a sense of status in the working class gave further strength to the organized labor movement. The sense of status in the worker was slowly awakened with the slowly pervading evils of industrialism. Thus if one concentrates on the underline social aspect of this revolution one finds that one of the most fundamental changes has been administrative technology which was made possible to exploit the new mechanical techniques. The administrative revolution has been characterized by more large scale organization and more administration. The growth of large scale industries and expanding economies gave rise to a new class of workers which we call managers. The expanse of bureaucracy found its natural successors in the managerial cadre. The number and the nature of technicians also yielded a variety of cadres; but in comparison to other workers those of the managerial and technical cadre were so highly placed in terms of salary that they refuse to regard themselves as proletarians. The growing complexity of technology on the one hand created classes of skilled technicians and managers and on the other hand vast masses of semi-skilled and unskilled labor. The technicians and managers since they refused to be treated as 'workers' they could not represent the aspiration of labor nor could they be accepted by the labor as their leaders. So a separate interest of the workers slowly emerged out of this. For the first time in management history, an organized labor came out into being. This was a prolegomena to the future trade union movement, so the existence of leader union created problems of social control which never existed before. A measure of their newness as well as the complexity of big business has been given birth to conflict between management and managers. The large size of industry has also profoundly changed the relationship between the entrepreneur and the employee from one that was predominantly economic to one that is primarily political and social. To discharge its responsibilities for the enterprise the management had to assume governmental authority over the members of enterprise. The emergence of the enterprise has radically altered the pattern of society by creating new classes broadly categorized under the new ruling group of executives and union leaders.

8. Labor Welfare

This period saw a continuous conflict for the first time between the management that was striving to protect its own interests and reap more and more profits, and that of labor which was fighting for its wages as well as struggling to improve its working conditions. The industrial labor movement derived its strength from the extreme optimism in human progress. This was also a morale booster for them. As a result, the idea of social reform was first mooted on the public platform and gained momentum in due course. The middle of the 19th century saw a considerable interest and activity concerning this social reform on a wide basis. The amelioration of workers conditions on social and political plane remained a main plank of the industrial development of this period. Thus industrial revolution was a revolution not only in technology but also in human relations. The conflict between capital and labor for profits and wages respectively continued to form a stumbling block in the way of smooth human relations. Not only this, but the vast complex of the organization made it necessary to develop an appropriate approach and the development of techniques to tackle human relations which were plagued with human suffering and exploitation of the workers. Moreover, factories were still run in a dictatorial fashion by entrepreneurs where machinery was the king and the human element in management was lost in the rush to take advantage of the fantastic gains in the productivity provided by new technologies. In effect, the technologist had the last word in managerial practices and managers sought to increase the output through a blending of all inputs entering into the production processes. The apathy towards labor aggravated their hardship. If unchecked, the apathy could perhaps have taken an ugly turn which could have been detrimental for the whole industry. It was necessary to get serious note of it in time.

Business and industry soon adopted scientific techniques and approaches to study and contain their problems and along with technological sophistication the human factor was more emphasized in struggling to meet these new problems. Managers adopted a whole series of new approaches generally known as scientific management emphasizing strictly formal organization of the bureaucratic type. The management growth of this new approach was greatly stimulated by the ideas of F.W. Taylor and his disciples.

9. Scientific Management

F.W. Taylor developed his concept of scientific management that was devised to measure the efficiency of the manufacturing operations. His concepts covered a broad field, including principles of management organization with emphases on production planning and scheduling. His work directly affected the factory labor as the application of the new scientific methods resulted in a systemic breakdown of jobs into elementary parts. In scientific management, managerial thinking began with one of the basic assumptions of orthodox and economic theory: that man is a rational animal concerned with maximizing his economic gains. If we assume that man's goal in the factory is to make money, then it naturally follows that management can get him to produce more if they pay him in accordance with the amount he produces. Thus the theory of economic motivation leads directly to the development of a piece work incentive system. In conclusion, the theories of scientific management were based upon standards, standard hours, standard machines, and standard workman and so on. Premise of scientific management is that there is one best way to do a job. This one best way will be cheapest, fastest and most efficient way to perform the task. While the process may not the safest or the most humane, it will allow the management to make the most 'profit' while scientific management did prove to be an effective management tool that increased the productivity of worker, it was criticized for treating the workers like a tool or machine and not like a person. It had a demoralizing effect on human and work environment. Human relations were most impersonal under this place.

10. Human Relations Movement

The next significant step in the development of human relations occurred in the late 1920 and early 1930's. The Hawthorne studies of Elton Mayo and Roethlisberger conducted their studies in the Western Electric Company, Chicago. Through these studies, they concluded that human interaction and attention paid to the workers by these researchers caused their productivity to increase: These findings were the first to indicate that social factors in the work environment could have significant effect on the productivity of workers. Fueled by these findings of the Hawthrone studies further research on social factors and how individual worker respond to them has undertaken. Results from these studies indicated that needs of employees must be understood and acted upon by the management in order for a worker to be satisfied; productive communication between the worker and his superior was stressed as was the need for a more participative work place atmosphere. It is interesting to note that the focus of the human relations era is now the backbone of more recent employee involvement that was found to increase the productivity of the workers along in the increase of the profits of companies adopted by them. The Hawthrone studies thoroughly examined the effects of social relations, motivation and employees satisfaction on factory productivity. The human relations movement viewed workers in terms of their psychology, and integrated them with the companies rather than having considered them as interchangeable parts. The hallmark of human relations theories is the primary push that needs to be given to organizations. Elton Mayo, further through his studies, stressed that natural groups in which social aspects take prudence over functional organizational structures, create upward communications through which communication becomes a two way traffic - from workers to management as well as vice versa. Cohesive and good leadership is needed to communicate goals and to ensure the effective and coherent decision making. Principles of human relations are:

- ❖ Human beings are not interested only in the financial gains. They also need recognition and appreciation.
- ❖ Workers need a high degree of job security and job satisfaction. Therefore, the management should give job security and job satisfaction to the workers.
- ❖ As organization work not only through formal relations but also through informal relations.
- ❖ Workers need high degree of job security and job satisfaction. Therefore, management should give job security and job satisfaction to the workers.
- ❖ Workers want good communication from the managers, therefore managers should communicate effectively without the feelings of ego and superiority complex.
- ❖ In any organization, workers do not like conflicts, misunderstandings among members of the organization.
- ❖ Workers want freedom. They do not want strict supervision. Therefore, managers should avoid strict supervision and control over workers.
- ❖ Employees would like to participate in decision making, especially in those matters affecting their interest. Therefore, management must encourage workers participation; thereby they will increase productivity and job satisfaction.

Throughout the ages, various valuable studies have been made but never before has there been consistent and continued investigation oriented towards the study of human relations in industry. It is Hawthrone investigation which focused a new concept of human relations. The school of human relations is people oriented as opposed to that of scientific management which was work oriented. The Human Relations approach has been defined as a science dealing with people at work. It recognizes that work is done by people usually in groups. It teaches us that the informal organization is a fact with which managers have to cope up with. The school further say that managers must find a way to get people to be committed to organizational goals, and one way to do this is to initiate communication from the bottom–up as well as from the top-down as well as laterally. Participation is still another way people should be allowed to be involved in the setting of goals, work standards and decision making. Hopefully, if we do all these things with the involvement of all workers, individual and organizational goals will become integrated. This recognition of the human relations school developed a clearer understanding of the human element and the result of this has been in the development of theories in the areas of motivation, coordination, participation, collaboration and leadership. Most of the early contribution of neo-classists has been primarily in the areas of organizational structure, participation of workers, better communications, job enhancements, job factors, work situations, group behaviors, group dynamics, leadership styles, decision-making, power and authority. All these studies have provided some insights into human relations at work. Thereafter, the spate of studies taking a clue from the Hawthorne studies continued to tackle human relations problems which resulted in one of the important studies of E. Jaque, done at the Glacier Metal Company on 'employee participation that is consultative hierarchy'. The study was designated for the following purposes

1. Providing worker representation in making decision on day-to-day operating problems as well as general policy
2. Improving communication between workers and management.
3. Giving all workers a feeling of a direct communication.

The management consultative hierarchy comprises a network of committees that represents all the interest groups in the organization, ie. work councils, representative committees, committee of executives, all of which are functionally inter-related to one another. This study brought out the nature of the democratic organization of the factory which was continually involving both the social and technical needs of learning. The fundamental principle behind all these discussions was that democracy means effective discussions which solve problems and get things done thereby giving everybody the opportunity to contribute through own's capacity, especially in terms of policy discussions. Another study of the participative scheme was done by Mocormick at the Mocramic Company, yet another study at the American Brake Shoe Company revealed that bottom- up management encourages and rewards those participants who take the initiative to suggest new and creative ideas involving work and work-related functions other than their own. Another important study in this field was at the Life Insurance Company done by Moore and Reimer while Rosen's study of a furniture company demonstrated how the workers involvement proved fruitful for increasing productivity.

These are classic studies in participative management, where human values such as individual growth and the employee's need to participate in the decisions to determine their positive relations at work.

11. Behavioral Science Contribution

Expanding the human relations school of thought through academic research in various other disciplines such as psychology, sociology, political science, economics and behavioral science resulted in the birth of a new era. Behavioral science focuses more on the total organization and less on the individual. It examines how the workplace affects the individual worker and how the individual workers affect the workplace. Modern day fields of organizational behavior (OB) focuses on the study of employee behavior in the organization; organization development (OD), the process of changing employee and organizational attitudes and beliefs as well as human resource management grew out of the Behavioral Science era. Supporting assumptions and observations researches came from many historical studies. The clash and conflict between capital and labor, the dysfunction of the bureaucracy, different leadership styles, understanding of individual motivation, teams and team working and group dynamics all sprung from the study of behavioral scientists. All these ingredients of man-management and organizational structures were accumulated into a coherent value foundation for the theory and practice of employee participation, involvement and empowerment. The combination of these factors was referred to as the Democratic Workplace or Industrial Democracy at work.

HISTORICAL STUDIES – A REVIEW

A chronology of events in today's democratic workplace right from 1926:

Mary Parker Fallet the management theorist and observer of labor – management relations in her article, "The Giving Oriers" advocated participative leadership and joint problem solving by labor and management. Much of her carrier was devoted to finding way to reduce adversarial relations between worker and management.

Chester I. Barnard in 1938 in his book "The functions of Executive," presented insight from his experience as president of the New Jersy Bell, Telephone company viewed organization as social systems that must be effective (achieve goals) and efficient (satisfy the needs of employees) His acceptance theory of authority proposed that authority is derived from the willingness of subordinates to comply with directions rather than from positions of power.

Lewin and Whyte in 1939, through their research work demonstrated that democratic leadership was superior to authoritarian leadership and laize-faire leadership in altering group climate and group performance. Democratic leadership seemed to bring out the best in the groups, while authoritarian leadership caused dependency apathy, aggressiveness and poor performance.

From 1940 to 1960, the Hawthrone studies triggered the human relations movement that advocated participative management, greater attention to social needs, training in interpersonal skills for supervisors and general humanizing of the workplace.

In 1948, Lestercoch in his article, "overcoming resistance to change" reported that resistance to change could be minimized by communicating the need for change and allowing the people affected by the participation in planning it.

In 1951, Carl Rogar's client – centred therapy demonstrated the efficacy of non-directive psychotherapy, which hold the capacity to assume responsibility for their behavior and mental health when provided with a supportive, caring social climate. Rogar's focus on effective inter-personal communication was applicable to superior – subordinate relations.

In 1960, Doglas M C Gregor wrote "Human side of Enterprise" in which he described his theory X and Y assumptions. Those who subscribe to theory X assume that people are lazy, dislike responsibility and self-centered and are indifferent to the need to be led. Those who subscribe to theory 'Y' assume that people have the potential to develop to assume responsibility and to pursue organizational goals if given the chance in an encouraging social environment. The task of the management is to change organizational structures, management practices and human resource practices to allow individual potentials to be released.

In 1961, Burn and Staker described two different forms of organization structure mechanistic and organic. In an environment of slow change, mechanistic organizations structure may be appropriate, in an environment of high change, an organic structures encourage decentralized decision making and authority, open communication and greater individual authority.

In 1961, Renis Likerts, "New pattern of Management" present data and theory showing the over whelming superiority of a democratic leadership style in which the leader is group-oriented, goal-oriented and shares decision making with the work group. This leadership style was contrasted with an authoritarian one-on-one-leadership style.

This short chronological review of studies captures most of the significant influences from researches, theories and observations utilized by industrial democracy practitioners. To summarize, intellectual enthusiasm for scientific management, bureaucracy, authorization leadership gave way to increasing doubts about these organizational practices as theory and research pointed out their limitations, dysfunctions and negative consequences. Out of these democratic thinking, employers, entrepreneurs, practitioners and academicians formulated a set of values and assumptions regarding people, groups and organization as humanistic, optimistic and democratic. The democratic values prompted a critique of authoritarian, autocratic and arbitrary management practices as well as the dysfunctions of bureaucracies. The humanistic values prompted a search for a better way to run organizations and to develop the people in them.

These historical studies on individuals, groups and organizations have some implications and assumptions about the studies on employee participation, involvement and empowerment. Two main assumptions are worthwhile to quote here are

1. Most individuals have drives toward personal growth and development if provided an environment that is both supportive and challenging. Most people want to develop their potential.
2. Most people desire to make and are capable of making a greater contribution to attaining organization's goals that most organizational environment permits.

A tremendous amount of constructive energy can be tapped if organizations realize and act on these assumptions. The implications of these two assumptions are very straight forward:

Asking, listening, supporting, challenging, encouraging, risk-taking, permitting failures, removing obstacles and barriers, giving autonomy, giving responsibility, setting high standards and rewarding success allow greater and wider opportunities of constructive problem-solving if all the parties in the system alter their mutual relationships in a positive and protective way. It is, then, possible to create organizations that on the one hand are humane, developmental and empowering and on the other hand are high performing in terms of productivity, quality and profitability. Putting people first certainly pays pay off handsomely in profits and performance.

Chapter 3

THEORISING THE ORGANIZATION

❖ Theory 'X'
❖ Theory 'Y'
❖ Theory 'Z'
❖ Transformation Strategies

Chapter 3
THEORISING THE ORGANIZATION

Changing the way we run the business means more than anything else changing the way people relate to each other in the way they work. It is true that an organization's behavior will not change unless acted on by the outside forces. Secondly, the resistance of an organization to change will be equal and opposite to the amount of efforts put into changing it and thirdly, the amount of behavioral change will be directly proportional to the amount of effort put into it.

Organizational change implies a massive change in its literal meaning, that is a change from one physical form to a quite different one. When we talk about peoples and organizations being transformed, we mean that some or all of their behaviors, opportunities, attitudes, values, cultures, characters, and commitments have undergone a rather complete change from the way they were before. Transformation that has taken place from an agrarian society to a global society always brought new thinking, new industries (services, hospitality) and new ways of managing, and even more important, leading the people who work in them. These organizations (under the assumptions of theory X, Y, Z) from the old economy who have gained from this cataclysmic change did so because they found superior new answers to their problems, and hence they will not re-track to their old and inferior management practices. The promises of organizational evolution and revolution in labor management relations provide a way of understanding the task of managing people and in bringing forth a new set of tools and techniques for talking that will enable those who will dare to transform the way they manage. In doing so, they will build their place in the winning organizations of the new economy.

While reviewing theories X, Y, Z, we have observed new changes in the assumptions of people and organization which are slowly carried out by organizational leaders. Changes in implementing organizational models in theories X, Y and Z demonstrated changes in people, leader behaviors, organization theorists, reformers, entrepreneurs, and this led to the gradual re-structuring of their organizations as per the changing mind sets of people and society at large. Intensive research studies of Dr. Dogulas Mcgregor; theory X, and Y and the theory of 'Z' of William Ouchi have very precisely enumerated the mindsets of people in a given situation and how they changed their thinking, behaviors, and their cultures at work. Now let us review the assumptions of these thinkers presented in the models X, Y and Z. This will help us to understand how organizations were theorized and how they practiced their organizational behavior. Theories 'X' and 'Y' advocated by Dr. Mc-Gregor and theory 'Z' is advocated by Prof. William Ouchi.

Assumptions of Theories and its impact on theorizing the organizations is taken here as briefly as possible.

Assumptions	Theory 'X'	Theory 'Y'	Theory 'Z'
1. Workers Motivation	Management assumes that the only motivation that works for employees is money.	Management assumes that employees are motivated by their needs to fulfill their social esteem, self actualization, and security.	Management assumes that employees are motivated by a strong sense of commitment to be part of some – thing worthwhile self actualization need.

2. Workers attitude toward employees	Management believes that the worker dislike work, avoids responsibility and seeks only security from work and their pay cheque.	Management believes that employees seek work as a natural activity and will seek out opportunities to have increased responsibility and understanding of tasks	Management believes that employees will not seek out opportunities for responsibilities. In fact they have opportunities to advance and learn more about the organization.
3. What will work with employees	Management believes employee will only respond to coercion, control and direction telling them exactly what to do or threatening punishment or firing.	Management believes that workers will respond best to favorable working conditions that do not pose threat or strong control.	Management believes that employees should learn the business through the various ranks only and that the organization will get the best benefits from employees by making it possible from him to have lifetime employment. The results will be strong bonds of loyalty developed in long term employment and shared responsibilities for decisions.

Both the theories Y and Z are characterized by participative style of management. Theory 'Z', Japanese style is based on the assumption that employees have a well-developed sense of dedication, moral obligations and self-discipline. They can make collective decisions through consensus. If you want to change your present organizational culture about man at work, then this theory may suit your organizational transformation. Dr. M.C. Gregor through his theory 'Y' concluded that employee participation consists basically in creating opportunity under suitable conditions for people to influence decisions which affect them. It is a special case of participation in which subordinates gain greater control, greater freedom of chance with respect to bridging the communication gap between management and the employees. This serves to create a sense of belonging among the employees as well as creating a conducive environment in which both employee and management would voluntarily contribute to healthy human and industrial relations. To conclude, both the contributors opinions, we can advocate that the significance of labor- management cooperation, which may vary from simple information sharing and consultation to employees participation, involvement can best be realized by contrasting it with the traditional form of control and management. Theory X of industrial enterprises states that contemporary organizations operate in the external environment which is characterized in an atmosphere of intense global competition coupled with technological innovation and change. This setting has stimulated a need for employees who can take initiative, embrace risk, stimulate innovations and cope with uncertainty. As a result, management has shown an enormous interest in employee participation with the belief that relinquishing centralized control will promote flexibility and decisiveness as well as employee commitment and subsequent improvement in individual and organizational performance.

TRANSFORMATION STRATEGIES

Those organizational leaders who contemplate changing the structures of their present organizational structures will find a tremendous source of support from Professor Ouchi who has prescribed 12 strategies to follow:

1. Trust will occur when both the parties understand each other views and know that both are doing it for the good of organization.

Everyone has to realize that with trust comes openness to say what you feel. People should have integrity. You should be able to treat the people the way you would like to be treated.

2. The organization should recast its philosophy, values and culture. Here organization will examine and audit how the organization is behaving with its employees and vice-versa. First the organization must understand its culture by studying decision made in the past. They will then have to organize a big meeting and ask themselves what they think worked and what they think was inconsistent. The answers to those questions bring out philosophy of the organization.

3. The management must be able to improve the organization leaders. Here, management cannot be intimidated by the management leaders and the organization leader must be willing to hear everything managers have to say. The organization leader must be willing to go into a detailed discussion with an open mind and to be able to trust his managers. When both began to trust each other, they are going to make easy decisions because both will be sharing information.

4. The organization will have to create both a structure and an incentive in the system in order to create a problem-solving situation so that whenever somebody ends up struggling with a problem, he can rest assured that his team will pick him up.

5. The organization will have to develop some inter-personal skills. Here, management is going to want everyone to improve on their communication skills. They need to encourage management to lay off employee but rather reduce their hours. This in turn will give the organization a low turnover rate that would result in a considerably less wastage of time in the training of new recruits.

6. The organization should design a system of slow evaluation and promotion and then develop individual potential and progress which will help to generate job security and a sense of long term employment.

7. The organization must broaden the employee's carrier path in order to retain employees within organization. Let them experience every job aspect and every department in the organization. Through this job rotation everyone will know what every department is doing. It makes much easier for the organization to pass important information within department.

8. The theory of 'Y' or 'Z' in working towards employee participation and involvement at the lower level needs to be initiated very patiently and cautiously with them. This is because the configured mindsets of the employees project a distrust of the management due to past negative precedents. Once this is established, only then can a positive patterned precedent be established by the management.

9. Find areas where employee participation is allowed in decision-making. The way you gain lower level trust is by allowing the employees' participation in the company's decision-making and to then give them rewards for their accomplishment. You need to encourage employees to speak and to let them know that the company wants them to work as a team and not as individuals.

While theory 'Z' has been called a sociological description of the humanistic organization advocated by management pioneers such as Elton Mayo, Charis Argysis, Rensis Likert and Dr. McGregor, in reality the descriptive phrase, theory 'Z', can be traced to the work of McGregor in the 1950s and 1960s. He presented a positive set of assumptions that he called theory 'Y' which was more positive about human nature as it relates to employees. In his view, the management which adopted the theory 'Y' beliefs would exhibit different and more humanistic characteristics and ultimately more effective management styles. His theory became the well known prescription for improving management practices.

Theory 'Z' of Prof. W. Ouchi advocated a modified American approach to management that would capitalize on the best characteristics of Japanese organizations and advocated its implementation could led to greater employee job satisfaction, lower rate of absenteeism turnover, high quality products, better overall financial performance within traditional American organizations. Theory 'Z' represents a humanistic approach to management. Although it is based on Japanese management principles, it is not purely form of Japanese management. Instead, theory 'Z' is a hybrid management concept approach combining Japanese and American management philosophies. Theory 'Y' is a largely psychological perceptive focusing on individual dyads of employer-employee relationship, while theory 'Z' changes the level of analysis to the entire organization. Theory 'Z' exhibit a strong homogenous set of cultural values that are similar to clans like cultures. Proponent of theory 'Z' suggests that common cultural values should promote greater organizational commitment among employees. The primary features of theory 'Z' are: long term employment, consensual decision making, slow evaluation and promotion, internal control with formalized measures, moderately specialized carrier path, holistic concern. Theory 'Z' incorporates elements that make it an even more participative style than theory 'Y.' Theory 'Z' is an alternative path of evolution towards participative management. According to theory 'Z', the very survival of an organization that adopts theory 'Z' depends on its ability to develop clans (teams) with the supportive management systems and philosophy. The step from going to 'Z' theory includes developing a new organizational philosophy, developing interpersonal skills, involving union, stabilizing employment, deciding on systems, enhancing employee participation, involvement and developing holistic relationships.

Theory 'Y' which stated that the work is natural and can be a source of stabilization when aimed at high order human psychological needs. Theory 'Z' focused on increasing employee loyalty to company by providing job for life with a strong focus on the well being of the employee.

Chapter 4

EMPLOYEE PARTICIPATION IN MANAGEMENT

- ❖ Origin of Employees participation
- ❖ Employee Participation-Perspectives-Economics, Social and Political
- ❖ What is Employee Participation?
- ❖ Forms of Employee Participation
- ❖ Pre-requisites of E-Participation
- ❖ Employee Participation – Managerial Concern
- ❖ Summing up-W.P

Chapter 4
EMPLOYEE PARTICIPATION IN MANAGEMENT

Today's organizations are moving towards more democratic processes, as they strive to improve their competitiveness by tapping the knowledge, skills and talents and creativity of their employees. Driven by global competition, technology and information tools, we see that means of production and services have shifted into the hands of employees. Autonomous work teams replaced managerial levels, scientific management theories have gradually given way to more participative approaches that stresses employees empowerment and involvement obvious

Early international efforts to regulate conditions of employees were done by International Labor organization right from 1919. The idea of regulating conditions of employees by an international treaty had progressively influenced the minds of many persons even earlier. Robert Owen, a social and industrial situation observer and reformer emphasized at the Congress at Philadelphia, the desirability of international regulations of labor in ensuring peace. In 1839, the French economist Blanqui observed that the primary purpose of treaties, instead of being to formed kill men, ought to preserve men's life and make them happier. In 1847, Daniel Legrand, a manufacturer, made an appeal to the Government of France, England, Prussia and Switzerland for enactment of international legislation for the protection of working class. In conclusion, the ideas of these pioneers influenced others and there was a widespread realization of the importance of international regulations of conditions of labor.

The outbreak of the 1st World War brought into light the existence of many important labor problems and it was realized that these should be solved only through the regulations by a permanent and active international agency. The trade unions which till then had been uncooperative to the international association for labor legislation also changed their attitude. In 1916 the General Federation of Trade Unions at its leads conference discussed several labor problems common to many countries and recommended the appointment of an International commission for the purpose of supervising and executing labor agreement. It also suggested the establishment of an international labor office for gathering materials concerning labor legislation. Public opinion was strongly in favor of the establishment of such agency. And on 31st Jan. 1919 the Paris Peace Conference appointed a labor commission which proposed the establishment of the International Labor Organization (ILO) and drafted its Constitution. Preamble to the constitution says 'whereas universal and lasting peace can be established only if it is based upon social justice, and whereas conditions of labor exist involving such injustice hardship and privation to large number of people as to produce unrest so great that the peace and harmony of the world are imperiled; and an improvement of those in urgently required; as for example by regulation of the hours of work, maximum working days and week, regulation of labor supply, the provision of adequate living wages, the protection of workers against sickness, disease and injury arising out of his employment, provision of old age, recognition of principle of equal remuneration for work of equal value, recognition of the principle of freedom of association, the organization of vocational and technical education and other measures; whereas also the failure of any nation to adopt human conditions of labor is an obstacle in the way of other nations which desire to improve the conditions in their own countries; the high contracting parties, move by the sentiments of justice and humanities as well as by the desire to secure the permanent peace of the world and with a view to attaining objectives set forth in this preamble agree to the… Constitution of the ILO.

Later on the Philadelphia Charter set forth a few fundamental principles at the time of inception. These few principles are embodied in the form of charter of freedom of labor, the most outstanding are:

- ❖ Labor is not a commodity.
- ❖ Freedom of expression and of association is essential to sustain progress.
- ❖ Poverty anywhere constitutes danger to prosperity everywhere.

The general conference of the ILO at its 26th session held in Philadelphia in 1944, re-affirmed these principles which were to inspire the policy of its members. The declaration popularly known as the Philadelphia Charter says: "Believing the experience has fully demonstrated the truth of the statement in the constitution of the ILO that lasting peace can be established only if it is based on social justice. The conference affirms that:

a. All human beings, irrespective of race, creed or sex have the right to pursue both their material well-being and their spiritual development in conditions of freedom and dignity of economic security and equal opportunity.

b. The attainment of conditions in which this shall be possible must constitute the central aim.

c. All national and international policies and measures, in particular those of an economic nature, are considered as all international economic and financial policies and

d. In discharging the task entrusted to it, the ILO, having considered all relevant economic and financial factors, may include in its decisions and recommendations any provision which it considers appropriate."

The conference recognizes the solemn obligation of the ILO to further, among the nations of the world, programs which would achieve.

a. Full employment and the raising of the standard of living;

b. The employment of workers in the occupations in which they can have the satisfaction of giving the fullest measure of their skills and attendance and make their greatest contribution to the common well-being.

c. The provision as a means to the attainment of this end and under adequate guarantee for all the concerned of facilities for training and the transfer of labor including migration for employment and settlement.

d. Policies in regard to wages and earnings, hours and other conditions of work calculated to ensure a just share of the fruits of progress to all and a minimum living wages to all employed and in need of such protection.

e. The effective recognition of the right of collective bargaining, the cooperation of management and labor in continuous improvement of productive efficiency and the collaboration of workers and employers in the preparation and application of social and economic measures.

f. The extension of social security measures to provide a basic income to all in need of such protection and comprehensive medical care;

g. Adequate protection for the life and health of workers in all occupations.

h. Provisions for child welfare and maternity protection;

i. The provision of adequate nutrition, housing and other facilities for recreation and culture and

j. The assurance of quality of educational and vocational opportunity.

One of the important activities of ILO is the creation of international standards of labor on various labor and social matters, covering conditions of work, industrial relations, social security, and labor administration. This helped in establishing uniformity in labor standards on a global basis, the influence of labor legislation and collective bargaining in many countries. (As a result of the activities of the international standards of labor, Indian labor legislation has been greatly and positively influenced. India has ratified some of the conventions adopted by ILO. The ratification of the conventions has put her under the obligation of implementing their provisions through their incorporation in labor laws and collective agreements.) The whole work of the ILO provides a stimulus to the ideal as well as to the legal cooperation of labor and capital. Gradually, employees received recognition as co-partners in industry. A kind of free atmosphere started emerging in which employees and management were both involved in decision-making processes legally and later on socially, economically and psychologically: The decision-making not only remained the only concern of the management alone but also involved the equal concern of the employees about the matters concerning them. Here, the origin of the worker participation concept emerged. ILO has paved a solid way for worker participation in management.

The main implications of the worker's participation in management as summarized by ILO are:

- ❖ Workers have ideas which can be useful.
- ❖ Workers may work more intelligently if they are informed about the reasons for and intentions of decisions that are taken in a participative atmosphere.

ILO is the foremost body on international labor issues and sets minimum standards of basic labour rights by formulating international labor standards through conventions and recommendations. With 179 member countries, the ILO can influence government and businesses through certain labor issues, thereby legislating international policies on the rights of workers. Such a broad role of the ILO has helped a lot in implementing worker participation in management in the majority of countries.

EMPLOYEE PARTICIPATION

Review of literature shows that the links between employee participation, company performance and quality of work life have three different perspectives of participation. These perspectives have different approaches for participation:

❖ Economic Perspective

Changes in the employees' attitudes and behaviors are achieved through financial participation of the employees by offering them a stake in the firm. They are made stake holders of the company by giving them company share holding rights. They are given bonuses, incentives and profit-sharing incentives pursuant to the profits of the company. These kinds of participatory values considerably enhance the importance of the employees at their work place and allow them the opportunities of self motivation and self importance to achieve the goals of company. This kind of participation is a kind of formal framework for the satisfaction of the employees. It seems that it has more formal recognition than social acceptance.

❖ Social Perspective

By catering to the needs of the employees for their job security, safety, health and insurance, a higher performance on the part of the employees may be expected by the organization. This will also ensure to enhance the improvement in the quality of the work life of the employees; this will undoubtedly and positively impact the quality of their social needs, thereby ensuring their satisfaction in this important area of their lives.

❖ Political Perspective

Recognizing trade unions as official bargaining agents of employees results in the approval of some rights that are equal to the management. The formation of such groups as work councils, joint consultation committees, works committees, a committee for the appointment of a workers' director on the company's Board of Directors, etc. constitute various types of participatory measures between management and labour that is expected to change the attitudes of the employees and to improve their work environment. Such types of participations seem to be more political and legal in nature.

Employee participation through these perspectives, though considered as a welcome step for the employees' 'say' in the business of management affairs, did not, however, yield much positive effect. It was observed that these potential participatory measures, designed to generate regular positive impacts on the employees, are effective only when these participatory measures are used in combination with such factors as financial and legal work-related matters, which maybe through direct or indirect participation. Either combination may act upon employee perception, encouraging them and thereby causing them to establish a high level of trust relations within the work place. This will further result in allowing the employees, with their different motivations, to enjoy the benefits of such participations. That is why a combinational approach of financial, social, legal, political and psychological work-related measures convincingly appears to have positive participation results.

True participation is possible only when employees at different levels have a 'say' in matters relating to their respective work areas as well as in decision-making that affects their performance. Only then will the total involvement of employees create a climate of participation that would encourage a sense of belonging and commitment to the team work in the organization. Therefore, the essence of true participation is as given below:

- ❖ Group identity, team work and interdependence
- ❖ A 'say' in decision making
- ❖ Greater/open two-way communication
- ❖ Better mutual trust
- ❖ Identification with organizational goals
- ❖ Better utilization of human resources potentials
- ❖ Better visibility and feedback to employees

Advocates of participative management believe that the vast majority of employees have the abilities, knowledge, skills and expertise to assume greater responsibility in work place and can make significant contributions to their organization; this enables them to satisfy many of their psychological and social needs through their work. It also means that the participatory nature and style of management stimulates employees enthusiasm, engagement and willingness to carry out decisions in which they are involved. Encouraging participation, satisfies employees inner needs and serves as motivating vehicle resulting in greater productivity, job satisfaction and effectiveness for the organization. Proponents of participation claim the participative management approach results in

- ❖ Increased employees satisfaction
- ❖ Higher employee morale and motivation
- ❖ Improved organizational performance
- ❖ Greater acceptance by employees of organizational change.

It is realized that business success begins with each individual in the organization and participation begins by involving and engaging everyone to contribute to business success. Therefore, an effective participation requires a sincere commitment to learn and assimilate new personal, professional, social and technical skills.

It has been for some time that organizations have been moving towards more democratic processes in workplaces as they strive to improve their competitiveness, knowledge acquisitions, skills, talents and the creativity of their employees. Driven by such encompassing factors as global competition, technology, information tools, etc., we see that the means of production and services have shifted into the hands of employees. Autonomous work teams have replaced managerial authoritarianism; scientific management theories have gradually given way to more participatory approaches that stress employee empowerment and involvement. Participative management techniques have reaped great benefits for industry in terms of productivity, quality and employee satisfaction.

Having considered the importance of participation, it is clear that employee participation (EP) is central to human resource management and modern organizational practices. Moreover, the benefits of Employee Involvement (EI) and Employee Empowerment (EE) are visible only if Employee Participation (EP) is implemented effectively.

WHAT IS EMPLOYEE PARTICIPATION?

"EP is defined as a process of employee involvement designed to provide employees with the opportunity to influence and where appropriate, take part in decision making on matters which affect them." It is a plural/collective approach with a continuum for 'no involvement to employee control.' As such, it may involve processes and mechanism such as collective bargaining, employee share schemes, work councils, joint consultation committees, works committees, workers' director on the Board of Directors, etc., obviously an employee has the right to question and influence organization decision making and this way involve representative democracy. EP is an act of sharing in something. It is therefore, joining with others in every activity that matters. It involves taking part in something and is more or less often supported by some rule and or legislation. Participation, however weather it involves having 'a say' in decision or sharing financial benefits, does not necessarily give employee (individually or collectively) any control over those decisions or the allocation of financial benefits. Although participating employees have potential influence within an organization, management is free to ignore their views and opinions if it so chooses. The employees' rights to fall in three broad areas: right to information, right to consultation and right to shared decision making.

Dachler and Wilpert (1978) identified four employee participation ideas/theories:

Democracy Theory	–	employees like politics; activate and release employees capabilities
Socialist Theory	–	Employees controlling production processes
Human growth and Development Theory	–	Employee participation lifts motivation and commitment
Productivity and Efficiency Theory	–	Employees raises productivity, efficiency, and quality of work, makes his mind to accept decisions.

While two theories have historically played a considerable role in the argument for more participation, there has been more emphasis on the later two over the past couple of decades. Nevertheless, the emphasis on employee rights has placed the democracy theory at the heart of most of the arguments for employee participation. Although there is a tendency to assume that employees want more participation, it is salutary to remember that employees are generally interested in participation as regards their own work. The productivity and efficiency theory has become more relevant as organizations try to improve their performances in the light of widespread organizational restructuring, which often make employees accept changes on important issues.

Out of these theories there emerged key concepts on workplace dynamics:

a. Employee participation in management – accesses to managerial information and having 'A say' in managerial decisions.
b. Employee financial participation-profit sharing, sharing ownership (Company share holding)
c. May or may not involve participation in management.
d. Financial participation is based on the idea that financial inputs lead to higher psychological commitments. It does not necessarily lead to greater work participation in management but may be employed alongside strategies for increasing workplace in management.
e. Industrial democracy – right to share power with manager. Industrial democracy is about governance, about power sharing in the workplace. It is related to collective power gaining with the implementation of legislative backed participation.

To recapitulate our decision, we may say workplace management is a system of communication and consultation either formal or informal, by which employees of an organization are kept informed about the affairs of the undertaking and through which they express their opinion and contribute to management decisions. It is industrial democracy in action based on the

Principles of equity, equality and voluntarism. It is distribution of social power in industry so that it tends to be shared among all who are engaged in the work rather than concentrated in the hands of minority. Thus the basic objectives of workplace management are;

- ❖ Democratization of management
- ❖ Personalization and humanization of management process
- ❖ Eliciting workers participation for achieving organizational goals
- ❖ Behavioral approach to the man management relations and so on.

These objectives are put into action by these forms of participation:

- ❖ Collective bargaining – joint decision making, consultation
- ❖ Informative and associative participation-

The right to receive information discusses and gives suggestions on the general situations of the concerned issues. For example, these issues cover the status of the market, production and sales program, circumstances affecting the economic position due to stiff global competition, long term expansion, modification, diversification plans etc.

❖ Consultative Participation

This involves a high degree of sharing of views of the employees and gives them the opportunity to express their feelings. Employees are consulted on matters such as welfare facilities, benefits, addition of new technology and the problems emerging from it, safety measures changed.

The workplace provides a way of direct participation to employees through such measures as team working, attitudes survey, suggestion schemes, indirect participation, collective bargaining, work councils, a committee appointed work director, joint consultations, etc. The push behind this direct and indirect participation is ideological; for individuals it means high expectations, attitudes towards authority, alienation and dissatisfaction at work, organizational change and improved human resource management.

It is all about power and centralization and how should the power and centralization be divided, the perspectives given in participation literature are: unitarist, pluralist and Marxist. It appears that it ought to be possible an employee's participation through pluralist, democratic processes where collectivized relations shares decision making and power.

Although participation techniques associated with participative management, employee involvement, and employee empowerment approaches appear to present differing views of participation, they shares a single, common line of inquiry. This includes all the various approaches to participation that are related and which share a common underlying dimension that represents different aspects of a more general process which can be referred to as employee participation.

Today everyone in the organization must be mobilized to improve the way that do their jobs and satisfy customers. To mobilize everyone to achieve these goals, organizations must change the way they think about the potential of their employees and to assist them to organize their work in a manner that allows them to participate and contribute. Employee participation is the only process that allows and enables employees throughout the organization to have an opportunity to plan, make and modify decisions affecting their work environment and their organization as a whole. In conclusion, successful employee participation relates not only to implementation of techniques alone but rather to the creation of an environment and the use of techniques within that environment.

FORMS OF EMPLOYEES PARTICIPATION

It is noticeable that many of these many of these forms of participation have been aligned with various management 'fads' and the popularity of participation schemes have varied considerably overtime. Participation of workers in decision making process has refused in successful value creation in many organizations. Though the extent to which employees should participate in organizational decision-making is still a matter of debate, some say that workers unions should participate with management as equal partners, while some believe in restricted or bounded participation, that is the participation of employees or workers to a limited extent. However, there are number of way through which employees can participate in decision making process of any organization.

1. Participation at Board Level

Representation of the employees at the board level is known as industrial democracy. This can play an important role in protecting the interest of employees. The representatives can put all the problems and issues of the employees in front of management and guide the board members to invest employee's benefits scheme.

2. Participation through Ownership

The other way of ensuring employee participation in organizational decision making is making them shareholders of the company. Inducing them to buy company shares, advancing loans, giving financial assistance to enable them to buy equity shares are some of the ways to keep them involved in decision making.

3. Participation through Collective Bargaining

This refers to the participation of workers through collective bargaining agreements/settlements by deciding and following certain rules and regulations. This is considered as an ideal way to ensure employee participation in managerial processes. It should be well controlled otherwise each party tries to make an advantage of the other.

4. Participation through Suggestion Schemes

Encouraging employees to come up with unique ideas can work wonders especially on matters such as cost-cutting, waste elimination, safety, reward system etc. Developing a full-fledged procedure can add value to the organizational functions and create healthy environment and work culture.

5. Participation through Complete Control

This is called self-management where workers/unions act as management. Through elected boards, they acquire full control of the management. In this style, workers directly deal with all aspects of management or industrial issues through their representatives. It is practiced in Yugoslavia.

6. Participation through Job Enrichment

Expanding the job content and adding additional motivators and rewards to the existing job profile is a fine way to keep workers involved in managerial decision making. Job enrichment, offers freedom to employees to exploit their wisdom and use their judgment while handling day-to-day business problems.

7. Participation through Quality Circle

A quality circle is a group of five to ten people who are experts in a particular work area. They meet regularly to identify, analyze and solve the problems arising in their areas of operation. Anyone from the organization, who is an expert in that particular field can become a member. It is an ideal way to identify problem areas and work upon them to improve working conditions of the organization.

8. Participation through Task Force

For identifying specific problems task force team is useful. It fits in with the focus on project management and incorporates a range of experiences in project teams.

9. Participation through Autonomous Workgroups

They are known as self-managing teams. It is always a key question how much teams are self-managing or weather key functions are managed from outside the teams.

10. Participation through Co-Management or Co-Determination

It is popular in German industries through work councils and employee director. It is also a hot discussion topic in European work councils as it constitutes an important management system in many of Europe's industrial organizations. Co-management is clearly a high level of employee participation – normally reserved to the term individual democracy and employee power can cover a range of issues.

11. Participation through Profit Sharing

It includes a draft of schemes designed to help employees share in the financial success of an enterprise. This is different from employee share holding since it only provides for a higher income flow. Generally speaking, profit sharing schemes are more common at the executive level than they are at shop floor level. Productivity gain sharing, however, is one way of applying a profit incentive to the entire workforce. Both profit sharing and employee share holding are used as part of pay-for performance packages. Productivity gain sharing is a more radical, comprehensive approach. It is linked with productivity and is indeed crucial.

All these various participatory schemes are fine-tuned and integrated in workplaces and these assist to consolidate the status of the employees in participating in managerial decision-making. Many organizations are quite comfortable and even supportive of such employee participation. Employee participation is a mental and emotional involvement of employees in group situation that encourages them to contribute to group goals and share responsibility for them. This entails three important ideas – involvement, contribution and responsibility. First and foremost, participation means managerial involvement rather than mere muscular activity or ego-involvement. Employee participation is that it motivates employees to contribute. They are empowered to release their own resource of initiative and creativity toward the objectives of the organization. Participation is more than getting consent for something that has already been decided. Its great value is that it taps the creativity of all employees. Participation essentially improves motivation by helping employees understand and clarify their paths toward the common goals of the organization. Finally, participation encourages responsibility in their group activities. It is a social process by which people become self motivated in an organization, they begin to say 'we' not 'they.' When they see a job problem, they say that the problem is 'ours' not 'theirs'. Participation helps them became good organizational citizen rather than non-responsible like machine – like performers. As individuals begins to accept responsibility for group activities, they see in it a way to do what they want to do, that as to accomplish a job for which feel responsible. When people want to do something they will find a way. Under these conditions to employees are ready to work actively with managers rather than relatively against them. The organization sees that employees are searching for a sense of significance, the opportunity to use their minds and a chance to devote their efforts to a higher purpose in their work. Meaningful participation can help satisfy these needs. In brief, the act of participation in itself establishes better communication as people mutually discuss work problems. Management tends to provide workers with increased information about the organizations finance and operations and their sharing of information allows employees to make better quality suggestions.

PREREQUISITES FOR PARTICIPATION

Participation works better in some situation than the others. And in certain situations it works not at all. Depending on socio-cultural values, norms and beliefs its results yield the fruits. Major essential areas of fruitful participation surveyed are as follow:

1. Employees must have time to participate before action is required. Participation is hardly appropriate in emergency situation. Base of positive and stable human relations must exist in the workplace.
2. The potential benefits of participation should be greater than the costs. For example, employees cannot spend so much time, participating that they ignore their routine work.

3. The subject of participation must be relevant and interesting to the employees, otherwise employees will work upon it merely as busywork.

4. Participants should have the ability of such vital factors as intelligence, knowledge, and skills to participate.

5. Participants must be mutually able to communicate with each other in the other's language in order to be able to exchange information and ideas.

6. Neither party should feel that its opinion is threatened by participation. If employees feel that their job security is at risk, they are less likely to participate fully. If managers feel that their authority is threatened, they will refuse participation or will be defensive.

7. Participation in any organization can take place only within the group's area of job freedom. The areas of job freedom are conditioned by certain parameters of discretions after all restraints have been applied. In no organization is there complete freedom, even for the top executives.

Employees want some control over things that affect them and some meaning in their work. Organizational leaders need to devote time to long-range efforts and to continuing discussions to promote participation as a means of encouraging human values which are needed at work. In such situations, participation has been so successful in practice that it has become widely accepted in more advanced nations and will soon become an important tool in the progress of developing nations.

MANAGERIAL CONCERN

Some managers/managements have some difficulty in adjusting to their new role in the participation and involvement systems. They still believe in theory 'X' organization culture assuming that employees prefer to be directed, wishing to avoid responsibilities, have relatively little ambition and more focused on their security needs. Secondly, they may fear losing their status as key decision-makers or may be concerned that they will have less power and control than previously. Those who are against the success of participative management in an organization reflect their failure to properly prepare their organization, their management and their employees for new emerging roles in an emerging empowered environment, and this stands as great obstacle to success. For a participatory management system, the management needs to start relinquishing their role of judge and critic and to begin viewing themselves as partners with employees. They need to communicate a direction for their industry to their employee workers, seek the help of the employees and to chalk up some challenging goals for the company with adequate monitoring resources. Hence, the management's new role is to view themselves as stewards of a broad range of human and technical resources. This stewardship paradigm shifts their emphasis from direction and control to that of servant leadership. While their challenges are to help others attain relevant goals while developing their skills and abilities. The essence of servant leadership is placing the needs of others above one's own self interest.

In spite of its numerous limitations, participation has generally achieved substantial access in the world of work. Participation is an important vehicle for empowering employees. Participation is the emotional and mental involvement of people in group situations that encourages them to contribute to group goals and sharing their responsibilities. It is a triumph for the employees and a positive psychological result of a supportive management. Groups in organization (teams) will likely to feel motivated and empowered when they:

- ❖ Share a sense of potency (have a can do attitude)
- ❖ Experience meaningfulness (have a commitment to a worth-while purpose)
- ❖ Experiencing genuine autonomy (having freedom and discretion to control one's resources and make decisions)
- ❖ See their impact on results. (can assess, monitor and celebrate their contributions and results)

These interactive contribution of these four forces can produce dynamic teams capable of being productive and protective as well as providing outstanding customer service – internal and external.

SUMMING UP

The three groups of managerial decisions in any management systems affect the employees of industrial establishment hence the employees must have say in it.

- ❖ Economic decisions – Methods of manufacturing, automation, shutdown, lay off, etc.
- ❖ HR decisions – Recruitment, selection, carrier progression, grievance settlement, work allocation, work performance, training and development and reward management.
- ❖ Social decisions – hours of week, welfare safety, health, environment, HR policies and procedures, salary and benefits and facilities.

Participation basically means sharing the decision-making power with the employees in an appropriate manner. The concept of a workplace is a broad and complex one inherent with cultural conditions and the scope and contents of participation changes from industry to industry and country-to country. Workplace management is the participation resulting from the practices which increase the scope of the employees' share of influence in decision-making at different tiers of organizational hierarchy with a concomitant assumption of responsibilities. ILO observes that workplace management may broadly cover all terms of workers associations and their representatives in decision-making, ranging from exchange of information, consultations, decisions and negotiations, to more institutionalized form such as the presence of member workers on the management's Board of Directors or even by the management workers themselves as practiced in Yugoslavia.

In the industrial world, change is the constant principle of today and to help people accept change employee participation is a must, because they produce quality products and services and they extend these services to the customers; they work on an organization's programs and profits. Unless your organization's employees are not given a share in decision-making, unless you promote the happiness of your employees and you cannot achieve operational aims. Unless you treat employees as internal customers, the ethics of your services and the quality of your products will not improve your market share. If you don't treat people well, you will have excessive turnover and won't be able to hire and retain best people.

In many Indian industries employees feel like they work in a dictatorship system. They feel that if they had more freedom at work, then their overall performance would improve. They would prefer this system rather than work in an atmosphere of fear and control in the workplace. Hence, increased participation, employee engagement as well as boosting the bottom-line results in the democratic workplace will enable them operate efficiently, consistently, and with excellent customer services, thereby making life better for their customers, employees, investors and families while also supporting their country.

An employee is a social being who brings his personality, hopes, aspirations, anxieties, feelings, and attitude to the workplace. He seeks satisfaction and meaning in his work as he does in other spheres of life. Through strict management control he tends to engage in naive behavior like absenteeism apathy, low commitment and low productivity. The Implication of these negative tendencies resulting from strict management control has therefore, raised serious concern among scholars interested in healthy industrial and human relations. Therefore, the rationale behind worker participation is anchored on the need to raise productivity level of employees through appropriate motivational techniques. The participation, involvement and empowerment of worker are considered as means for motivating them leading to positive work attitude and high productivity. Workers participation has been seen as capable of providing workers with conducive work environments and opportunities to exercise their innate potentials and willingness to pursue corporate goals of the organization. Worker participation has been explained as plank of industrial democracy. Where it is occurring, industrial democracy affects the nature, control and even ownership of private enterprise, the nature, control, power and bargaining areas of the trade unions and the role and contributions and rights of the industrial worker in contemporary and future industrial society.

Employee participation may be determined by number of different factors.

- ❖ The belief that the national culture in which the organization is located which influences level of participation.
- ❖ The belief that the characteristic of the business, specially the level of competition and the percentage of employees that belongs to trade unions will affect the amount of participation.
- ❖ The belief that an organization's size and business strategy will be related to the level of participation management that an organization adopts.

Worker participation must be examined in multidimensional constructs. Participation is an arrangement which involves workers making decisions sharing responsibilities and authority in workplace. Participation increases productivity and service delivery from more effectively from fully engaged and happier work forces. Other benefits of WP include less industrial disputes resulting from better and open communication in the work place. Improved and inclusive decision-making processes results in qualitatively better work places. Participatory decisions decrease stress and increases well-being. It also increases job satisfaction and improves the sense of fulfillment. Workers participation is not just a legal, social or economical discipline to plough a sense of 'a say' in workers mind but it is a culture with its own values, objectives, beliefs, tools and language. To conclude, we must say that participation provides relationship behaviors because employees are involved and empowered to make decisions. They decide how and when to perform tasks and also know how to perform them. When employees are able and willing to perform their tasks and are confident in doing so, then the delegation of job assignments and decisions of tasks becomes simple and effective.

It is possible to create organizations that on one hand are human, developmental and empowering and on other hand are high performing in terms of productivity quality and profitability. Evidence for this assumption comes from numerous examples (organizational experiences worldwide). Where "putting people first" paid off handsomely in profit and performance.

Any organization's base rests on management philosophy, values, etc., as well as the culture and vision of the employees. It is imperative to note that employee perception to see this as quality of work life directs their degree of motivation. It is, therefore, supportive, interactive, collaborative and participative in culture and, hence, must exist in the organization. Organizational leadership with supportive orientation turns employees as partners in progress. Drivers of employee participation and involvement consist of leaders who want to see the change and who also have the ability to communicate the new direction to employees. This makes a big difference for the pursuance of the employees' participation. Leaders consider that employees also have a voice and realize that their employees are their business partners. For the organization to enjoy the returns from employee participation, involvement and empowerment, the leadership must diligently work to create the environment where it is obvious to all that the employees' participation is desired, wanted and cultivated. It is the management's responsibility to create the environment for the employees' participation. It is, of course, true that you get only what you give.

The recent "push" of increased competition and the "pull" of new opportunities, both very much driven by advanced technology, make full utilization of human resources necessary. Employees must be encouraged to take the initiative to decide, to act and to learn in real time. This means embracing shared values as a guide to behavior. As speed, quality and productivity become even more important, organizations need people who can instinctively act in the right way without instruction, and who feel inspired to share their best ideas with their employers. This means letting go of some the managerial/supervision control in order to obtain on results. The participated, involved and empowered employee ultimately acts like the one who is self-employed with the responsibility for both, result as well as career. In fact, the motivation comes from within and is based on needs for self- efficiency. Employees feel empowered when they feel a sense of influence, competence, meaningfulness and choice. This is the power of transit motivation associated with a commitment on an internalized desire to take personal responsibility for work efforts and results. When commitments are obtained from employees that are aligned with the organization's core ideology, a significant amount of authority can be given to those on the front line for responsiveness to customers, both internal and external.

In short PIE processes are enabling or authorizing processes to individuals and groups to think, behave, take action and control work and decision-making in autonomous ways. It is the state of feeling self-empowered to take control of one's own destiny. PIE is a developmental strategy for individuals, teams/groups and the organization as a whole.

Chapter 5

EMPLOYEES PARTICIPATION IN MANAGEMENT (IN THE INDIAN CONTEXT)

❖ Employees Participation in Management – In India
❖ Gandhiji's Trusteeship Philosophy
❖ Employees Participation – Legal Framework in the Indian Context

Chapter 5
EMPLOYEE PARTICIPATION IN MANAGEMENT (IN THE INDIAN CONTEXT)

As a result of international standards of labor, Indian labor legislation has been greatly influenced. India has ratified some of the conventions adopted by the ILO. The ratification of the conventions has put her under the obligations of implementing their provisions through their incorporation in labor laws and collective agreements. The second National commission on labor appointed by government of India on October 1999 submitted its recommendations on June 2002 covering major points of the ILO on labor matters and accordingly Indian labor laws were amended and reframed.

One of the important recommendations of the NCL was the workers' participation with management. Workers and management need to join together not only to sort out their day-to-day problems but also to build confidence with each other by improving their work cultures, ensuring the introduction of new technologies, improving production processes, achieving production targets, smoothening retrenchments and introducing new technologies to make the enterprise capable of standing up to global competition. With the onset of globalization, the time has come when we cannot leave the question of participation to be determined by the management or the trade unions. We believe, therefore, that it is now urgent that the government enact a law to provide for participatory forums at all levels, keeping in mind the necessity to ensure that the responsibility and freedom to make managerial decisions are not fragmented to the detriment of the enterprise, the social partners or society at large.

In India, by passing the industrial disputes Act of 1947 under which works committee, joint council, grievances handling provisions, were inserted. The industrial resolution of 1956 also emphasized the need of associating workers with management. It says, "in a socialist democracy, labor is a partner in the common task of development and should participate in it with enthusiasm. There should be joint consultations of workers, technicians; Enterprises in a public sector have to set up an example in this respect." The concrete shape to the concept of labor participation in management was given in the second five year plan and the government of India announced its policy as, "It is necessary in this context that the worker should be made to feel that in his own way he is helping to build a progressive state. The creation of industrial democracy therefore, is the perquisite for the establishment of a socialist society." The approach of the planning commission was accepted by the government and parliament and towards the end of 1975, the government announced a scheme for workers participation in industry at the shop floor level as a part of its 20 point programme. Encouraged by this new scheme the workers' participation in management was announced in commercial and service establishments, manufacturing areas, management of public sector undertakings and nationalized banks. The finance minister, Prof. M. Dandwate, while presenting his first budget for the National Front Government in the year 1990, intended to give the workers a share in the ownership of public sector enterprises in order to secure their full participation in management. Out of this participation initiatives following things are expected from both the parties. While reviewing the whole history of workers participation in India, these issues are getting highlighted for its necessary implementation:

1. An atmosphere free from psychological inhibition on both the sides – labor and management must be created and with mutual cooperation nothing is impossible. There should be a complete mental revolution and both the parties should change their attitudes in a positive manner towards each other. Both should

agree to cooperate with each other in implementing decisions that are agreed upon to increase production and payment of fair wages and as well as in allowing benefits to the maximum possible extent, in the interest of the industry and society.

2. Representatives of workers and management in bipartite and tripartite committees on the Board of Directors should be trained in the mechanics of participatory schemes so that they may give a good thought to the proposals put before them and to suggest something concrete for the betterment of the industrial unit.

3. There should be only one representative union and multiplicity of union should be crubed by legislation. Secondly, union leadership must be from within and not from outside. This way union can be strengthened.

4. Communication gaps must be eliminated, suggestion schemes, joint consultative and committees should be formed at the plant level to discuss mutual plant issues between the workers' representatives and management representatives.

5. Communication gap must be eliminated, suggestion scheme, joint consultative committee to be formed at plant level to discuss plant issues mutually between workers representatives and management representatives.

6. Wide publicity to worker participatory scheme must be given for the knowledge and understanding of workers through lectures, discussions, film shows, conferences, seminars and other methods of propaganda in order to create awareness and importance of the participation.

7. Participation must be considered as complementary to collective bargaining, which will create conditions of work and legal relations on fair and reasonable man-management.

8. Industrial peace and productivity must be ensured by avoiding unnecessary stoppages of work in way of strike or lockouts, as their presence ruins the workers, harms their good interest and interest of society at large and put workers to financial losses.

9. Progressive personnel/labor/HR policies in respect of recruitment to retirement should be implemented in order to ensure workers' retention for their growth within the industry.

10. The follow-up action on the decisions of the participative bodies should be ensured. The government should also set-up a machinery to act as a watch-dog for implementing the scheme.

It requires change in the mind-set, attitude of both the parties. The public sector companies should initiate such schemes as a model employer and guide to the private sector for its implementation.

Since the implementation of the scheme in public sector undertakings in India, workers/unions are now matured and have a better understanding than before. It has been experienced that in the industries where the schemes are implemented, the efficiency and productivity of workers have increased and labor relations have been greatly improved. This has led to a higher sense of responsibilities among the workers in the first instance and so they should be given an opportunity to gradually participate at the plant level at higher and higher levels. But for a successful implementation, it is a prerequisite that both management and workers should adopt and attitude of positive thinking. If the scheme is implemented honestly it would benefit all parties concerned. i.e. employers, employees, society and country.

We can now summarize the broad objectives of workers participation in management.

1. It is an instrument for improving efficiency of the enterprises and establishing harmonious relations.

2. It is a device for developing social education for collective solidarity among workers and for tapping latent human potentials through getting workers suggestions and improving attitudes towards work and the organization.

3. It is a means for attaining industrial peace and harmony leading to higher productivity and increase profitability.

4. It is a humanitarian act for giving the workers an acceptable status within the working community and a sense of purpose in work activities.

5. It is an ideological point of view to develop self-management of self and industry where they work.

The foremost objective of the workers' participation is the achievement of the economic objectives of the organization by improving the productivity and profit as well as in improving industrial and human relations. The destructive attitudes of workers/unions are replaced by constructive and rational thinking. The worker participation system takes into consideration the maximum economic welfare of the organization instead of focusing narrowly on the maximization of profits as the sole definition of industrial prosperity. Legitimate right to share the gains of higher productivity of the enterprise. The purpose of workers participation scheme is to get the worker respectable status. It assures the human dignity because they become partners in the gain of productivity. The workers participation scheme also brings a change in the attitudes of workers. They consider themselves as part and parcel of the plant; they develop a kind of ownership with their work, their workplace, with the people and the organization. Workers will accept their responsibilities in an activity because they feel themselves the partner in taking the decisions on the matters concerning them and they will see how it is being implemented. Participation makes them responsible employees. It satisfies their economic, social, and psychological needs and help in raising the level of motivation, belongingness.

GANDHI'S TRUSTEESHIP PHILOSOPHY

On trusteeship Gandhi's said, "Rich people can earn crores by all means. But understand that wealth is not yours. It belongs to peoples. Take what you require for your legitimate needs, and use the remainder for the society." The truth hitherto has not been acted upon; but if the moneyed classes do not even act on it in these time of stress they will remain slaves of their riches and passions and consequently of those who overpower them. The laborer has to realize that the wealthy man is less the owner of his wealth than the laborer who is the owner of his own, eg. the power to work. Therefore, those who owned money are now asked to behave like trustees holding their riches on behalf of our poor. You may say that trusteeship is a legal fiction, but if people mediate over it constantly and try to act upon it, then life on earth would be governed much more than it is at present... absolute trusteeship is an abstraction and equally unattainable. However, if we strive for it, we shall be able to go further in realizing a state of equality on earth than by any other methods. If capitalists do not become trustees on their own accord, force of circumstances will compel reform unless they court utter destruction. Working for economic equality means abolishing the eternal conflict between capital and labor. It means a leveling down of the wealthy few in whose hands is concentrated the bulk of the nation's wealth. In one of the construction worker's conference at Madras (Chennai), Gandhiji replied that "economic equality of his conception did not mean that everyone would literally have the same amount. It simply meant that everybody should have enough for his own needs. For instance, the elephant needs a thousand times more food than the ant, but that is not an indication of inequality. So real meaning of economic equality was: to earn according to his need. We seek not to destroy the capitalist, we seek to destroy capitalism. Therefore, we invite the capitalist to regard himself as a trustee for those on whom he depends for the making of retention and the increase in capital. So the laborer need not wait for his conversion. If capital is the power so is work. Either power can be used destructively or creatively on the other. The laborer realizes his strength and he is in position to become a co-sharer with the capitalist instead of remaining a slave. If he aims at becoming the sole owner, he will most likely be killing the hen that lay the golden eggs."

To summarize Gandhiji's trusteeship concept, we may pin-point six point formula as essentials of his trusteeship:

1. Trusteeship provides a means of transforming the present capitalist order of society into an egalitarian one. It gives no quarter to capitalism, but gives the present owing class a chance of reforming

itself. It is based on the faith that human nature is never beyond redemption;

2. It does not recognize any right of private ownership of property, except in so far as it may be permitted by society for its welfare;

3. It does not exclude legislative regulation of ownership and use of wealth.

4. Under state regulated trusteeship, an individual will not be free to hold or use his wealth for selfish satisfaction or his disregard of the interest of society;

5. Just as it is proposed to fix a decent minimum living wage, a limit should be fixed for the maximum income that would be allowed to any person in society. The difference between such minimum and maximum incomes should be reasonable and equitable and variable from time to time, so much so that the tendency would eventually be towards obliteration of differences.

6. Under the Gandhiji's economic order, the character of production will be determined by social necessity and not by personal whims or greed.

From the above review of trusteeship concept it is clear that worker participation in management is relevant to trusteeship concept. If we consider capital as power, so is the work of the laboring masses. If this power is used creatively it will be a healthy sign of co-partnership in industries, where either is dependent on the other. Therefore, the mainstay of industry's economy is deeply rooted in workers' participation which should be relevant and correct. People learn and are willing to learn only when what is being taught them is linked with what they do every day. We must examine their cultural, social and psychological background. Participation is the business of education and training to dispel doubt, fear and frustration and to remove suspicions of people in particular segments of the working classes. Participatory education on involvement and participation must help the worker to grow strong, healthy, energetic, and ethical by building up both their mental and physical faculties. In fact, the modern industrial world requires not only good educated employees but also great qualities of head and heart. Generally, this is required in all areas of industrial life through different forms and styles but special training, skills and abilities are necessary to understand and tackle the complicated problems of modern industry and trade. Worker participation if properly educated, implemented and practiced shall be the most potent means for the full development of human resources. Here, then, making worker participation legal stands secondary. (Ref. quality through trusteeship, 1978, by Vadilal L. Mehta, Mumbai).

In summary, the theory of trusteeship propounded by M.K. Gandhi is based on three principles:

- ❖ Human Karma
- ❖ Samanta (equality)
- ❖ Swaraj (Self-management)

An example in downright discriminatory exploitation is when an owner of a property uses his superfluous wealth for the well-being of his employees but neglects the well-being of those who are unable to take care of themselves. This concept can best be contrasted in the joint family system, where head of the family possesses all property but uses it for well-being of all members.

Trusteeship is the natural answer to modern management science. It establishes healthy and lasting relationship between employee, employer and management. In the strict sense of the term it is not just an article of business management but an ideology, which by its very nomenclature implies a determined sense of dedication and commitment for social purposes, as was advocated by a band of enlightened industrialists in India during the first of the 20th century under the leadership of M.K. Gandhi.

The concept in essence is a paradigm shift in the mind set of the entrepreneur, industrialist or CEO, who considers himself as trustee in the management of a given organization on behalf of all involved. In this case, the "social good" becomes the role and goal of the leader of an organization's management.

WORKERS PARTICIPATION-LEGAL FRAMEWORK – IN THE INDIAN CONTEXT

What was assumed, till now, to exist automatically is sought to be promoted today deliberately and consciously. Labor-management cooperation, workers participation in management and joint consultation have all become words of legal meaning. The areas of most common interest comprise labor and management such that they may cooperate consciously to the advantage of both in the promotion of efficiency, productivity, eliminating of waste, reducing costs and in improving quality of products. In a word, it is in the common interest to increase the size of the cake, so that each of the parties may have larger pieces as its share. It is on such issues that many schemes of the workers' participation have been founded. The method can be established on the basis collective bargaining or legislation. It is collective bargaining that sets the term on which participation/cooperation takes place in the field of common interest, thereby guaranteeing each its proper share in the fruits of participation.

Workers' participation in management (WPM) is also advocated as means of promoting industrial democracy. It is said that workers should have a voice in the management of the enterprise to which they belong. This will lead to the achievement of industrial democracy which is a logical corollary of political democracy. Work under such conditions would become a source of satisfaction. As political democracy is supported, even though it may not be the most efficient way of organizing the affairs of a community, industrial democracy is therefore emphasized, though it may not necessarily lead to increasing the efficiency and productivity of the enterprise. Hence, the workers' participation in management is advocated to ensure that industrial democracy, for its own sake irrespective of its influence, is more or less favorable as regards the economic efficiency of the enterprise.

There are three important aspects of promoting workers participation

   a.   Increase in efficiency and productivity of the enterprise,
   b.   Creating and maintaining industrial democracy; and
   c.   Preserving industrial peace.

Workers participation in management (WPM) may take various forms and may be of different degrees: information sharing, problem solving, joint consultation and participation. Under this form, the process of decision-making becomes really joint and bipartite. Both the union and management have a say in decision-making and they also undertake responsibilities for the result of their action. Workers participation in management in many cases imply a representation of the workers on the Board of Directors of the company, or it may simply mean the establishment of joint councils of representatives of management and workers. These councils are vested with the power to take final decisions on matters entrusted to them, either on the basis of bargaining or legislation. The emergence of collective bargaining has enabled workers and unions to share the decision making power of the management in many areas of administration of an enterprise. Wages, working conditions, hours of work, dismissals, promotions, lay-offs, retrenchments, job evolutions, health, safety, and welfare and many other related matters are decided on the basis of collective bargaining.

Workers' participation in management in India has primarily been a government sponsored movement. Section-3 of the Industrial Disputes Act, 1947, empowered the state and central governments, in their respective jurisdictions, to make general or special orders regarding the employer of an industrial establishment employing one hundred or more workmen in order to constitute a working committee.

Joint management councils, unit councils and joint councils in commercial and service organizations in public sectors, under ID act 1947, have elaborate machinery set ups. Working Committees, joint councils, shop floor committees, conciliation officers, Conciliation Boards, Courts of Inquiry, Labor Courts, Industrial Courts, National Tribunals, all these authorities are empowered to conciliate, mediate and arbitrate to make references and to pass court decisions respectively when labor management cooperations are dysfunctional in their operations. These are some of the different forms of workers' participation management in Indian industries.

Besides this, suggestion schemes, establishments of quality circles etc., are also available. Workers' participation in the true sense also mean working in private sectors like TISCO and other many private sectors. Today, every industry is having workers' participation management in a formal way or informal manner.

Chapter 6

EMPLOYEE INVOLVEMENT IN MANAGEMENT

* ❖ What and Why of Employees Involvement
* ❖ Benefits of Employees Involvement
* ❖ Employees Involvement – Ford Company Model

Chapter 6

EMPLOYEE INVOLVEMENT IN MANAGEMENT

WHAT AND WHY OF EMPLOYEE INVOLVEMENT

"It is generally conceded in the liberal democratic world that working people should have right to participate in the making of decisions which critically affect their working lives." (R. Ban 1994)

The radical democratic school of thought stems principally from the politico-philosophic traditions of British Guild Socialism, German social democracy, Europeans anarcho-syndicalism and Indian Gandhiji's trusteeship concept, which all have endeavored, in thought and action, to make the concept of industrial democracy the central element of a new economic order in which production is dictated by social needs and managed under the control of employees. For these movements industrial democracy is primarily associated with a profound reordering of existing work relations to control over the employers wishes and will.

An organization needs to maximize its employees potential if it wants to be successful in competitive business world. Involvement is regarded as providing solutions to the age-old problems of Taylorism and bureaucratic work places where creativity was shuffled and employee became alienated, showing discontent through individual and collective means. A message was the need to move away from the hard rationalist model of scientific managment to more initiative style of management "Productivity through people" and entrepreneurship. The message was that successful organizations focused on managing culture.

Secondly, the globalization created important momentum for a re-establishing and strengthening employee involvement in different forms: information, consultation and participation in the management.

Thirdly, one of the underlying reasons for the present crises is that the labor law system has failed to act as counter veiling power to restrict to increase in economic inequality and union decline. Strengthening the power of workers by giving them capabilities for making their 'voice' hard might help rebalance the system. That is why employees involvement is important for the reasons:

- ❖ To strengthening work place democracy, enable dispute resolution and a social dialogue at the work place.
- ❖ Give a strong 'voice' to those with a long-term interest in the organization.
- ❖ Ensure that information on what is going on in the company reaches the management.
- ❖ Act as a whistle blower vis-à-vis the authorities to report unethical behavior at work places.
- ❖ Check excessive level of top executive pay and facilities.

Guaranteeing local representation is good for productivity and well-being of workers and that a well functioning participation system can create a win-win situation. Employee involvement is creating an environment in which employees have an impact on decisions and actions that affect their jobs. Employee involvement is rather a management and leadership philosophy about how people are most enabled to contribute to continuous improvement and ongoing success of their work organization. Employee involvement increases ownership and commitment, retain your best employees and fosters an environment in which people choose to be motivated and contributing. The means and methods of Employee involvement are suggestion systems, establishment of manufacturing cell, work teams, work improvement teams, kaizen teams, quality improvement teams, task force etc. Intrinsic to most Employee involvement processes is training in team effectiveness, communication, problems solving, reward and recognition systems and frequently the sharing gains made through Employee involvement efforts. Employee involvement is a series of strategies an organization can adopt to allow employee more responsibility and accountability for preparing a product or offering a service. The term itself can refer to a wide range of practices from simply soliciting employees work improvement ideas in small group with manager to self-managed teams, who are given total control over their jobs and working environment. Also in the concept of Employee involvement is the idea that unions or other employees represented groups should have the power to participate in the factory and company level decision making process. Employee involvement thus based on two principles.; the first is that people tend to support what they helped to create,-second, underlying Employee involvement idea is the idea that people who know most about the inner functioning of an operation are those who actually perform the work. Asking for involvement and participation of employee actually performing their jobs can provide insight not available from managers or consultants. Therefore, one of the key components of successful implementing Employee involvement is open and truthful communication among and between employees at all levels of the organization.

Some of the benefits of Employee involvement are experienced by practicing (Employee involvement) organizations are:

BENEFITS OF EMPLOYEES INVOLVEMENT

1. Employees involvement provides a greater understanding and acceptance of decisions by subordinates because the subordinates are involved in making those decisions.
2. Similarly, employees who have 'a say' in the decision are more committed to implementing it.
3. Involving employees in the decision making and planning practices of the organization provides a greater understanding

of the organization's objectives and improves commitment to achieving these objectives.

4. Employees involvement provides greater fulfillment of psychological needs and therefore, it provides greater employees satisfaction.

5. Employees involvement can capitalize on the social pressure other members will place on fellow employees to comply with the decisions the group made as a whole.

6. Employees involvement provide a greater team and organizational identity which is shown through greater cooperation and coordination among members at all levels.

7. When conflicts do arise under Employee involvement situation, the employees involved are better able to constructively deal with it.

8. Employee involvement produces better and balanced decisions.

"Two heads are better than one," the team concept has been catching on from Employee involvement on shop floor to higher level of corporate-executives. Self-managed teams and quality circles are coming together to solve their workplace problems voluntarily. The suggestion system is the fore-runner of workers participation and involvement. Thus, employees feel they have increased sense of their true abilities when their ideas are deemed good enough to be implemented by their company. Employee involvement was largely a utopian ideal shared by only few true believers. However, today it is a bonafide movement with an extremely large following. Employee involvement has been openly welcomed by manufacturing, service, hospitality sectors alike a way to improve commitment, quality, productivity and customer service and satisfaction through people in the work place.

FOUNDATIONS FOR EMPLOYEE INVOLVEMENT

Therefore, the organization must select best people –

Motivation comes from within an individual. Therefore, if you hire the people who have potential to be motivated half of the battle is win. Use Pygmalion effect-if you truly believe in your employee, they will believe in themselves. Take the time to psychologically invest in your employees. Recognize contribution-provide public recognition for employees who have performed well. Be sure to be consistent about when the rewards are provided. Provide incentives and rewards. Remember that psychological reward of the incentive is often greater than the monetary reward. Also incentive can be a useful motivation in the short-term. Empower employees-make employees responsible for the company's products and services. Listen to what they have to say and use their ideas. Invest in your employees just as you would invest in new equipment. When employees are recognized, appreciated and are put in charge of reaching goals, they generally reached it. By providing them information, encouragement and engagement, employee would realize that they are important part of the company business. This helps develop ownership with the organization.

EMPLOYEES INVOLVEMENT-FORD COMPANY MODEL

Employee involvement pays rich dividends in terms of employee and organizational effectiveness when implemented with commitment and conviction. Ford employee involvement implementation model is considered on most pragmatic and systematic intervention that brought many benefits and laurels to the company. Ford Company follows following steps in this model.

1. **Local management trade union agreement** – This is considered essential for positive organizational change and the involvement of employees at every level.
2. **Local joint employee involvement steering commitment** – A local joint group is formed which meet regularly. The members are also given training on effective group process soon after their inclusion in this committee.
3. **Briefing employee on Employee involvement** – Steering committee members conduct these briefing sessions. These sessions are conducted in small groups to facilitate discussion.

4. **Selection and appointment of Employee involvement coordinator** – He is appointed by joint steering committee internal to the site selected from interested applicants. The coordinator's role is to support and later to train problem solving groups and to provide a link between them and the rest of the organization.

5. **Information gathering and diagnosis** – A number of techniques are used in data collection and diagnosis that include-interview with sample workplace; managers and trade union representatives dealing with the perceptions of the site. Second interview is conducted by the third party consultant and finally data is fed to coordinating committee and then to workforce.

6. **Employee involvement Training** – Awareness workshops are conducted for mixed groups of middle management and union leaders exploring Employee involvement in depth are conducted. Skill training workshops are also conducted for problem solving subjects.

7. **Problem solving group launches** – These groups are launched at all levels of the site organization, involving all the employees.

8. **Monitoring and support of groups** – This process includes coordinators and consultant meeting with problem solving groups and continued training and coaching, on leadership and facilitation.

The above model is of great practical value to all those organizations that intended to follow suit. However, before jumping into this band wagon managers must answer the key question of what they intended to achieve through Employee involvement and must develop an implementation plan like that of Ford Company.

Chapter 7
EMPLOYEES EMPOWERMENT

- ❖ **Introduction to Employees Empowerment**
- ❖ **Meaning, Purpose, Contents and Dimensions of Employees Empowerment**
- ❖ **Components of Employees Empowerment**
- ❖ **Effectiveness of Employees Empowerment**
- ❖ **Guidelines for Management/Managers on Employees Empowerment**
- ❖ **Elements, Values and Attributes of Empowered Company**
- ❖ **Employee Empowerment – Concluding Observations**

Chapter 7
EMPLOYEES EMPOWERMENT

An employee is one of who works for a business or another individual for pay. Employer can mean giving legal authority to act or promoting the actions of another by giving them the means to do so. Employee Empowerment does not to be a formal strategy for business, though it has became just that in recent years. For example, an individual business owner may empower an employee simply by telling him that he trusts the work will be done properly. When the task is completed, the owner/manager then support what an employee has accomplished to complete the process. This is called Employee Empowerment in traditional way. The term Employee Empowerment currently defines a managerial style that allows non-management staff to make decisions without having to get the approval of a manager. In this system of empowerment the organization with a formal process will probably define which tasks and which decisions can be made without upper level inputs.

Employee Empowerment represent the most recent manifestation of involvement practice. Until recently 1990's; the empowerment was virtually unheard of within industrial relations circles. In their in depth study conducted by Michigan Univ. researchers identified the form of combination of involvement elements and the latest offering with magical properties to secure the missing link between employee commitment, engagement and bottom-line performance. Later on in one of the Harvard Business articles which promoted empowerment as a principal agent to transform control-oriented organizations to commitment-oriented organizations in response to competitive pressures. Empowerment has its origin in social and educational psychology where it retains a fairly precise meaning as a strategy for individuals to retain control of key aspects of their lives. Until recently, however definitions of empowerment have received little or no attention in academic and HRM literature. Now it has diffused and taken up in two distinct ways:

- ❖ As an individual strategy for the manager, based on attaining personal success through restructuring his attitude.
- ❖ As a collective strategy for the organization in the sense of a realization or devolution of decision making power to those who do not currently have it.

The later meaning is clearly part of wider motion of commitment. It appears to be the approach to empowerment which has gain most currently today. Interest in enhancing employee commitment as a strategy for effective organizational performance to replace the traditional Taylorist (scientific management) emphasis on control over employees, was induced by culture created by the successful penetration of European and American market by Japanese Companies. Japanese 'single status' in canteen or other facilities using fascinated European and American companies. More so, they quickly focused their attention on the Japanese organization of production, especially 'lean' or just-in-time system work was perceived to be high level commitment given to the Japanese company by its employees, posing a question of how to endanger a similar mind-set in conventional western labor market situation.

Employee Empowerment in any process that provides greater autonomy to employees through the sharing of relevant information and the provision of control over factors affecting job performance. Empowerment helps remove the conditions that cause powerlessness while enhancing employee feelings of self-efficacy. Empowerment authorizes employees to cope with situations and enables them to take control of problems as they arise. For viable empowerment following broad approaches can be followed:

❖ **Helping employees achieve job mastery** – giving proper training, coaching and guided experience that will result in initial successes.

❖ **Allowing more control** – giving employees discretion over job performance and then holding them accountable.

❖ **Providing successful role models** – allowing them to observe peers, who already perform successfully on the job.

❖ **Using social reinforcement and persuasion** – giving praise, encouragement and verbal feedback designed to raise self-confidence.

❖ **Giving emotional support** – providing reduction of stress and anxiety through better role definition, task assistance and honest caring.

When management uses these approaches, employees begin believing that they are competent and valued, that they have meaning and impact and they have opportunities to use their talent. In effect when they have been legitimately empowered, their efforts are more likely to pay-off in both personal satisfaction and the kind of results that the organization values. Mutual goals setting, job feedback, modeling and contingent reward systems are some of the goals available to management to attack employees' feeling of powerlessness. Various programmes, projects for participative management provide employees for verifying degrees of perceived ownership, inputs to various steps in the decision making process, and the key feeling of choice in their work environment.

EMPLOYEES EMPOWERMENT – MEANING, PURPOSE, CONTENT AND DIMENSION

Empowerment is one of the most effective ways of enabling employees at all levels to use their creative abilities to improve performance of the organization they work for, and the quality of their own working life. Employee empowerment is a kind of the risk management process whereby a culture of empowerment is developed information in the form of a shared vision, clear goals, decision making boundaries and the result of efforts and their impact on the whole is shared, competency in the form of training and experience is developed, resources or the competency to obtain them when needed to be effective in their jobs, are provided and support in the form of mentoring, cultural support and encouragement of risk taking is provided. (Chaturvedi, 2008)

Employee Empowerment – Definition

Fundamental reason to difficulty in making all purpose definition of employee empowerment is difficult because of its multi-dimensional concept (that involves a dynamic process in a dynamic environment and many elements that have role in different phases of this concept). Therefore, inconsistencies may remain in the conceptualization of empowerment.

Psychological empowerment most typically describes four factors that comprise empowerment: meaningfulness competence, choice and impact. Social structural empowerment (samad) describes power sharing, power distribution, information sharing, knowledge, rewards, self-esteem, leadership and organizational structure are the important controllable determinants of employee empowerment. When aspects in social structural characteristics received by employees are perceived as capable of fulfilling their positive, emotional state by being more empowered: Employees who perceive high level with social structural characteristics are more likely to feel empowered if they perceived with proactive personality. Thus for employee empowerment psychological and social structural factors and proactive personality traits are important factors in influencing employee empowerment. The complexity of the construct of employee empowerment confounds many organizational attempts to increase it. In order to be sustained, empowerment needs to be part of long term strategy of the organization. Empowerment initiatives should be guided by the dual objectives of improving organizational effectiveness and improving the quality of work life for employees. Too often employee empowerment have been viewed as a simple way to motivate employees to do more. Ethical issues and long-term effects on employee must become part of the landscape for our empowerment efforts.

The following definitions, it is hoped will emphasize the purpose and different dimensions of employee empowerment are: According to Kanter(1977) and other authors empowerment is to give power to people who are weak in organization. Empowerment is spreading the administrative responsibility to all the places in the organization. Empowerment is to give more authority to employees in management of work. It is to bring employees to the position of owners of work. According to Foster, Fishman and Keys, it is a process of bringing an individual or a group to a position that he can affect events and the results (Hanold-1997). According to Rothstein (1995) empowerment is "an act of building and increasing power through cooperation, sharing and working together."According to Pet and Miller, employee empowerment is the concept of enabling subordinates to have authority and capacity to make decisions and to act for the organization in order to improve both individual motivation and organizational productivity. A more operational level and process-oriented definition of empowerment is offered by Brow and Lawler. They define empowerment "as sharing with front-line employees the information about an organization's performance, information about rewards based on the organization's performance, knowledge that enables to understand and contribute to organizational performance and giving employees power to make decisions that influence organizational direction and performance." According to Murrel, empowerment is an act of building, developing and increasing power by working with others, which he terms as 'interactive empowerment' and having the ability to influence one's own behavior, which he calls on self-empowerment.' According to Cenger and Kanungo "empowerment is a process of enhancing feelings of self-efficiency among organizational members through the determination of conditions that fosters powerlessness and through their removal by organizational adjustments." From the above definitions we can summarize that employee empowerment is a process to satisfy the internal and external customers through increase employees' authority in the work and their knowledge, skills opportunities, self-confidence and desire related to their authority also, it is a process of providing perception related to this increase.

Employment Empowerment Purpose – The purpose of empowerment is to increase the authority, knowledge, motivation related to work of employees; thereby to enhance the contribution of employees to the organization and customers satisfaction. At the same time to increase the self-respect, confidence and loyalty towards organization. In short, the aim is to increase the satisfaction of the internal and external customers.

The Content of empowerment – As the empowerment can be done at individual level; it can be done at a team level which in size contains all employees in a process, in a unit or in the organization.

Employee Empowerment Dimensions – An empowerment from top-down or from manager-employees means giving power to employee at four dimensions that consists of authority, specialization, resource and personality.

❖ Authority is the power dimension which makes up the essence of empowerment or the body. The power dimension are the characteristic which uses authoritative power effectively, supportively, easily and complementary. The authority dimension of empowerment, the right to take decision related to the meaning, the environment and content of the work done by employees.

❖ Specialization dimension, the knowledge and skills of decision making, its application.

❖ The resource dimension – the most important sharing of knowledge, the possibility of attaining and using resources related to their work;

❖ The personality dimension-are self-confidence, self-esteem and the use of authority and motivation. Some of the main factors that determine the empowerment perception are: meaning-finding the work done by the employees as meaningful and important; competence-to feel oneself as sufficient.

Self-Determination – The possibility of making choice and impact – the degree of effectiveness perceived over certain results in the work process. The qualities of employees, who will be empowered, are important organizational and managerial atmosphere are the principal variables of empowerment. The encouragement and motivation to decision making by managers to their subordinates; creating a participation culture and creation of a sharing vision; emphasizing flexibility and autonomy, sharing information, inspiring confidence and the level of managers trust to their subordinates are some of the supportive variables for successful employee empowerment.

Based on employee empowerment meaning, its contents and dimensions, now we can evaluate what employee empowerment strategies to be developed. Following are some of the strategies (in brief) which can benefit employee empowerment in the organization.

- ❖ Change in work definition – The content of the work (to increase activities the required of work) or authorization by widening the meaning and framework; determining new jobs which suitable for vision and mission of the organization; by enrichment, rotation methods thus to increase authority of employee and meaning of job.
- ❖ By enlargement the span of control, to facilitate authority transition from managers to subordinates.
- ❖ By increasing the qualification of the managers with training programmes, recruitment and selection systems and to facilitate and encourage authority sharing manager's with their subordinates.
- ❖ By increasing qualification of employees with recruitment and training and to support and facilitate effective use of authority and to increase and support, confidence in the managers for the sharing of authority; to encourage the subordinates to take over authority.
- ❖ By applying in organization the team basis, on the basis of cooperation and interaction and to provide empowering of employees improving and increase positive interactions
- ❖ By restricting the work process, to increase influence on the eork process and its results on employees.
- ❖ By benefitting from performance measurements to help employees foresee their weak/strong features and to increase their power in the areas they use their authority.

❖ With rewarding system based on performance to motivate the employees for using authority getting and sharing knowledge.

ESSENTIALS OF EMPOWERMENT

Empowerment is one practice that can be realized only through a systematic plan persistence and commitment of management as well as employees. John Nihols (Empowerment in organization 1995) narrated following essentials;

1. Get the basis rightfully using current capability-empower people to the fullest extent of their current capability within the scope of their job tasks. A bottom-up training based approach might work better setting more modest-objectives and getting the basics right first, before going into the big picture. Delegate authority in the job tasks to make optimum use of employee capability is first step in empowerment.

2. Stretch people beyond their current capability to fulfill their potential. This is possible when managers will act on coach and enablers.

3. Widen empowerment by creating commitment throughout the organization. Once first and second stages are completed, the foundations should be laid for a change of attitude and behavior in the organization as a whole. As people are involved in wider activities, well beyond their continued job tasks, their broader understanding and growing range of activities transform their capability. Here, the manager begin to realize that by letting go of authorization power they gain the power to energize people achieving results beyond expectations holding them accountable for outcomes.

   - **Providing successful role models** – Allowing them to observe peers who already perform successfully on the job.
   - **Using social reinforcement and persuasion** – Giving praise, encouragement and verbal feedback designed to raise self-confidence.
   - **Giving emotional support** – Providing reduction of stress and anxiety through better role definition and honest caring.

When management uses these approaches, employees begin believing that they are competent and valued, that they have meaning and impact and they have opportunities to use their talent. In effect when they have been legitimately empowered, their efforts are more likely to pay off in both personal satisfaction and the kind of result that the organization values mutual goal setting, job feedback, modeling and contingent reward systems are some of the goals available to management to attack employees' feeling of powerlessness. Various programmes, projects for participative management provide employees with varying degrees perceived ownership, inputs to various steps in the decision making process and the key feeling of choice in their work environment.

COMPONENTS OF EMPLOYEES EMPOWERMENT

Empowerment opportunities are limited when employees perform routine, repetitive production or service job. There is more potential for meaningful job and self-determination in jobs that have complex tasks and enriching job characteristics.

1. Job design and Motivation

Customer service jobs are more empowering when the business strategy allows customized and personalized attention and employee have longer interactions and continuing relationships with the same customers. Therefore, jobs that are designed with only technology in mind are not supportive of empowerment. Socio-technical systems designed with flexible technology encourage employee empowerment. Five characteristics are essential to all jobs in order to have intrinsically motivating work: (Hackman and Oldham – 1980)

Task identity is the degree to which the individual performs a whole piece of work.

Task significance is to which the jobs has a substantial impact on the lives of others.

Skill variety is the degree to which the job requires different skills of workers.

Autonomy is the degree to which individuals feel personally responsible for their work.

Feedback is the degree to which the job provides information on level of task accomplishment.

These five characteristics of jobs contribute the three critical, psychological, states in the individual: he experienced meaningfulness of the work; experienced responsibility for outcome of work and knowledge of actual results of work activities. As a result employee experiences intrinsic motivation when the work generates these three psychological states.

COMPONENTS OF EMPLOYEE EMPOWERMENT

Empowerment opportunities are limited where employees perform routine, repetitive production or service job. There is more potential for meaningful job and self determination in jobs that have complex tasks and enriching job characteristics.

1. **Job Design and Motivation** – Customer service jobs are more empowering when the business strategy allows customized and personalized attention and employee have longer interactions and continuing relationships with the same customers. Therefore, jobs that are designed with only the technology in mind are not supportive of employment. Socio-technical systems designed with flexible technology encourage employee empowerment. Five characteristics are essential to all jobs in order to have intrinsically motivating work: (Hackman and Old ham-1980) task identity – is the degree to which the individuals performs a whole piece of work. Task significance-is the degree to which the job has a substantial impact on the lives of others. Skill variety – is the degree to which the jobs requires different skills of workers. Autonomy-is the degree to which individuals feel personally

responsible for their work. Feedback – is the degree to which the jobs provides information on level of task accomplishment. These five characteristics of jobs contribute to three critical psychological states in the individuals: he experienced meaningfulness of the work; experienced responsibility for outcome of work, and knowledge of actual results of work activities. As a result employee experiences intrinsic motivation when the work generates these three psychological states.

2. **Participative Leadership** – Participation can be encouraged and facilitate by involving employees when making decisions that affect them: Involving employee can potentially improve the quality of decision making in the workplace and it helps to improve the acceptance of decisions and employee satisfaction with the decision making process. Consultative decisions, joint decisions are made together by the leaders and other relevant parties. Delegation gives an individual or group the authority and responsibility to make decision.

3. **Organization structure, Reward systems, and Access to information** – Centralisation can limit the opportunities for managers to use job enrichment and delegation with direct reports. Decentralization organizations that compete on the basis of customized products and services provide more opportunities for employees to take initiative in determining how to do the work. Building more democratic organizations means redistributing power to all levels in the organizational hierarchy. Empowerment is increased by employee access to information, materials, funds and facilities needed to do the work effectively. Employees that have more access to information about the mission and performance of the organization experience more empowerment.

4. **Organizational culture and empowerment values** – Shared beliefs, and norms, values held by members of an organization are known as organizational culture. A supportive culture that values employees and their contributions facilitates empowerment. Creative problem solving is supported by an organizational culture

with strong values for information, sharing fair and constructive judgement of ideas and reward and recognition for new ideas. In contrast, a culture that only emphasizes traditional approaches and avoidance of mistakes discourages creative problem solving.

5. **Employee skills and traits** – The responsiveness of employees to opportunities for more responsibility and participation is greater when they have a high level of achievement motivation, high self-confidence and self-efficacy, and an internal locus on control orientation. In general, employees with higher level of education, tenure of job level report experiencing more feeling of empowerment. An empowerment intervention increases job knowledge substantially in less experienced employees rather than more experienced employees. Organizations that invest in building employee skills, achievement, orientation and self-confidence can increase the livelihood of successful empowerment.

6. **Leader selection and Assessment** – Regardless of the method of leader selection (team leader, term limit), influence in greater and more empowerment occurs when member participate actively in assessing leader performance.

7. **Replacing the old hierarchy with self-managed teams** – More responsibility is placed upon unique and self-managed teams which create better communication and productivity. Employees feel they are autonomous to make decision. By allowing employees to be autonomous, it helps to build trust between employer and employees. Use of authority and responsibility, maximizes all-round work efficiency and ownership with job.

Employee empowerment is considered by many organizational theorists and practitioners to be one of the most important and popular management concepts of modern time. Organizations ranging from small to large and from low-technology manufacturing concerns to high-teen software firm have been initiating empowerment in attempt to enhance employee motivation, increase efficiency and gain competitive advantages in the turbulent contemporary business environment.

EFFECTIVENESS OF EMPLOYEE EMPOWERMENT

Despite some notable success, many organizations experienced failure results of employee empowerment efforts. Initially they get attracted by a fantasy version of empowerment and simultaneously repelled by the reality. In one of the studies in UK, only 461 reported substantial performance gains through employee empowerment. Reasons for failure are many from industry to industry. But following are some o the possible reasons of failure in general.

- ❖ Empowerment demands change-command and control approach used by manager do not yield expected gains from employee empowerment. True empowerment requires that managers relinquish some of their control to employees. Managers need organizational support and training without that employee empowerment can't be implemented. Managers sometime are afraid of that employee empowerment may reduce their power and exalted status as heroic leaders.

- ❖ Empowerment is slow moving process-change from a command and control to employee empowerment requires a commitment to long-term change. Too, often, management fads and quick fixes in the name of empowerment have been implemented rather than relevant changes in management systems, structures, cultural values, norms and beliefs. To be successful, empowerment must be seen as a long-term program of employee participation and involvement.

- ❖ Employees' resist change-Decision making and influence are part of the political power system in organization. And employees generally get conditional over the years to follow orders, not collaborate with management. Getting greater responsibility employee fear insecured. They feel taking initiative and contributing to be the bigger picture in the operation may induce fear in them.

- ❖ These are the potential reasons for not getting the potential benefits as expected. Top management support for major changes in the organization is most warranted. We remain hopeful of successful employee empowerment because there are organizations around the world, who embrace principles of employee empowerment. The common denominators that these organizations are they involve employees in decision making, reward employees fairly, and provide training and career opportunities. As a result, these organizations demonstrate higher productivity than employees in comparable low-pay and followers on command-control systems. When employees have the opportunity to participate in decision making, training profit sharing and stock ownership, they are more productive and this productivity offsets costs for higher salaries and benefits.

Guidelines for Management/Managers-Despite mixed reviews of empowerment efforts at organizational level, there is real evidence that suggests the organizations can achieve benefits from empowering their employees. Research on participation, involvement suggested some of the following guidelines for management leaders to make employee empowerment feasible:

- ❖ **Identifying appropriate situation** – This primarily involves as assessment of the importance of decision, the relevant participants in the decision, the likelihood of cooperation and acceptance of the decision.
- ❖ **Management must-support employees** – People must be encouraged, involve to speak up, to express their concerns and ideas. One strategy is to describe initial propels as tentative, and to solicit opinions on ideas as they are formulated.
- ❖ **Good listening skills** – It is the first requirement of employee participation and involvement. Managers must learn how to elicit ideas from everyone, even who are hesitant to speak up. They must learn to express sincere appreciation for the inputs of others, in order to build an environment of participation.
- ❖ Manager must involve employee in the decision making that will ultimately affect them, an employees will have more interest

in getting involved in matters of importance to them personally. Managers need to take into consideration the individual differences in the employees in their shop floor/office, as variability in ability and motivation will impact involvement. Providing excess to relevant information and resources will contribute to the likelihood of successful employee empowerment. Removing unnecessary bureaucratic controls and constraints will ease successful completion of tasks. Lastly, managers need to use multiple sources of information and frequent checkups to be sure that their empowerment initiatives truly result in employees feeling empowered. Empowerment initiatives must be guided by the dual objectives of improving organizational effectiveness and improving the quality of work life for employees. Ethical issues and long-term effects on employees must become part of the landscape for employee empowerment efforts. (Ref-Gary A.Yukl and Wendy S. Becker, organization management journal-2006).

ELEMENTS OF EMPOWERED ORGANISATION

Employee empowerment is a beyond bureaucracy challenge. People oriented organizations who are genuinely fit for use of human beings, by extending free and inspiring work environment are the high performing organizations. They are the organizations making more inspiring and engaging work atmosphere available to their employees; where every employee is aligned by a deeply felt sense of purpose and where management assumptions and practices inspire and unleash their imagination, initiative and energy from all corner of the organization. These organizations are managing without managers. I mean they are replacing manager-management culture and practices with more alige self or peer management and consequently replacing rigid hierarchy with the creation of a new social systems of organizations.

Empowered employee organization centers on the three important concepts: communication, willingness to serve and common purpose. Profitability term now a day changed to maximizing corporate value, and it is abundantly made obvious by high performing organizations that it is empowered employees who achieve the goals. To accomplish goals they think it is essential that the corporate culture be robust and led by leaders, not managers. They understood the difference between manager and leader. They say manager administers, leader innovates, the manager maintains, leader develops, the manager relies systems, the leader relies on people. The manager counts on control, the leader counts on trust, the manager does things right, the leader does the right things. (W. Bennis). The psychology of profitability and the maximization of corporate values lie within the culture of the organization and through communication, willingness to serve common purpose, organizational culture can be maximized, as can wealth, as long as the culture has a solid business decision. It is believed that people in organization are the only true agents in business. All other assets and structures-whether tangibles or intangibles are the results of human action,(KarlSveiby). All depend ultimately on people for their continued efforts and existence, values unless consistently maintained, nourished and improved erodes overtime. Since individuals are the change agents they must be consistently maintained, nourished and improved through common purpose and willingness to serve. Empowered employees organizations have a belief that a clear vision and value proposition understood and worked on by all employees with regular reminders, updates and reinforcement makes a lot of difference. Setting practical, achievable goals and mile stones cascaded throughout the organization and commitment to follow through is the magic formula keeping people united and undisturbed. The empowered companies ultimate objective is to develop flexibility and encourage continuous improvement through its people-both management and employees to be aware, to think, to accept change, to voice suggestions for change and improvement and to implement them.

Employee-centred organization is thus the by-product of such thinking. They establish a world-wide presence in one or more activities, adopt a world-wide strategy and develop an outlook that is focused on the world as a whole rather than on nations or borders. Leaders of such organizations ensure alignment of everyone's efforts through focus on shared purposes, shared values and distinctive capabilities that turn vision into reality. This entails a fundamental shift in thinking about how to deal with people at all levels of old hierarchy-from command to align, from control to enable, and from manage to lead. Employee empowering organizations have created democratic workplaces and are part of most successful companies today because they enable an innovative, learning and collaborative environment at the work place.

VALUES OF EMPLOYEE EMPOERED ORGANISATIONS

Gallop study survey findings identified six values with corresponding practices imbedded in an organizational culture developing full potential of their employees. Their values are:

1. **Self-responsibility** – Individuals take responsibility to have their job, team function the way they wish to be. This that counter points to bring a victim within an organization.

2. **Authentic communication** – Individual communication is open, honest, transparent. Individuals talks about real issues going on in the organization.

3. **Trust** – Individual feel safe enough to try out new behaviours and take risks without fear or reprimand or put down by their superior or colleagues if they make mistakes. There is a genuine sense of good will that pervades the organization.

4. **Learning and growing** – Individuals are encouraged and rewarded to work on the real growth issues necessary for professional and personal development within the framework of the organization. Individuals are ever challenging themselves and supporting each other to develop and grow.

5. **Personal and group process skills** – Individuals and organization establish protocols and develop skills which are regularly developed to resolve inter-personal issues that come up in project management. Such issues resolved quickly and clearly.

6. **Caring** – The organizational leadership demonstrate in tangible way, concern for employees well-being. Employees feel valued and are inspired to give their very best efforts on behalf on the organization.

Such organization believe that the essence of empowerment is to release, rather than under-utilizing employees experience, initiative, knowledge and wisdom. Employee's performance is a major factor that leads to the success of business.

EMPLOYEE EMPOWERMENT – SOME CONCLUSIONS

Employee empowerment is a two sided coin. For employees to be empowered the management leadership must want and believe that employee empowerment makes good business sense and employees must act. One thing is clear that employee empowerment does not mean that the management no longer has responsibility to lead the organization and is not responsive for performance, if anything is opposite is true. Strong leadership and accountability is demanded in an organization that seeks to empower employees. This starts with the executive leadership level and includes all management levels and frontline supervisors. It is only when the entire organization is willing to work as a team then the real benefits of employee empowerment are realized. For the organization to practice and foster employee empowerment the management must trust and communicate with employees. Employee communication is one of the strongest signs of employee empowerment: Honest and repeated communication from elements of the strategic plans, key performance Indicators (KPI's), financial performance, down to daily decision making. If an organization is not cultivating employee empowerment, it may make considerable time and efforts before employees start to respond. When considering employee understanding and acceptance of decisions, consider how long it takes for the management team to discuss and then make decision. For an organization to enjoy returns from employee empowerment, the leadership must diligently work to create the work environment where it is obvious to all that employee empowerment is desired, wanted and cultivated. Management's responsibility is to create the environment for employee empowerment.

It is our strong conviction that most organizations demonstrated by the amount of communication, level of training provided, employees opportunities for personal growth, the solicitation and implementation of ideas, the recognition and reward systems, promotion and advancement criteria and unaccountable little signals from management that demonstrate whether employees are valued or not. Management has the obligation to create the environment that fosters employee empowerment, employees have the duty to accept the opportunity and demonstrate that they are willing and capable. This will benefit to organization as well as individuals and teams. Through employee empowerment the organization will harness individual talents to the full change the manager's mindset and leaves them with more time to engage in broad-based thinking, visioning and nurturing. The teams become more enthusiastic, active and successful. This will facilitate team work and harnessing of collective power of employees.

Employees are the important asset of today organization. Especially in the new knowledge economy, independent entrepreneurship and initiative is needed throughout the ranks of the organization. Involvement in an organization is no longer a one-way street. In today's corporate environment a manager must work towards engaging organization forcefully enough to achieve its objectives. New knowledge-based enterprises are characterized by flat hierchial structures and multi-skilled workeforce. Managers assume more leadership and coaching tasks and work hard to provide employees with resources and working conditions they need to accomplish the goals they have agreed to. In brief, managers work for their staff and not the reverse. Employee empowerment is the oil that lubricates the exercise of learning. Talented and empowered human resources is becoming the prime ingredient of organizational success. A critical feature of successful teams, especially in knowledge-based enterprises, is that they are invested with a significant degree of empowerment or decision making authority. Cross-level work teams can contribute a lot to corporate decision making and planning participatory management means seeking employee's opinions and action whenever possible and keeping an open mind to the suggestions and criticism they offer. Through participatory management approach following benefits are visible.

- ❖ **It works on powerful motivator** – You own what you do and where you work.
- ❖ **A trusting climate is created** – It is important for all employees to knoe not what is being done, but why.
- ❖ **Employees understanding their jobs better** – As they understand better how they fit into achieving the overall goals.
- ❖ **Better decision results a synergy effect from collecting more inputs.**
- ❖ **Progress towards corporate goals** is accelerated through frequent discussions about how the work is progressing.

Getting the best out of employees is above all a product of the 'softer' side of management. How individuals are treated, inspired and challenged to do their best work and the support, resources and guidance that is provided by managers to help make exceptional employee performance a reality.

Chapter 8

EMPLOYEE'S PIE – AN APPROACH

- ❖ Participation, Involvement and Empowerment – Effect
- ❖ Pie – A Collaborative Intervention
- ❖ Pie – Perspectives – For Leader, Employee and Organization
- ❖ Pie – Difference in Meaning

Chapter 8
EMPLOYEE'S PIE – AN APPROACH

Organizations today are trying to tackle the uncertainties of today's world by drawing out the creative potential of the people who are the organization. PIE are the means and methods for creating an organizational environment where people are equipped, encouraged and empowered to make decisions in autonomous way and feel that they are in control of the outcomes for which they are responsible. PIE are the processes of building trusting relationships among management, employees and customers. While reviewing the literature on PIE at least three primary attributes are seen in common. They do not cause PIE directly but they are considered to be requirements for successful PIE:

- ❖ **Supportive Management Culture** – A receptive and supportive organizational culture in the first attributes required for PIE. Supportive group based belief system and peer based support is required for implementing PIE.
- ❖ **Inspirational Leadership** – Inspirational and committed top leadership is identified as necessary for a successful PIE in any organizations.
- ❖ **Inter-personal Trust** – Mutual trust is the critical attribute for PIE work. Teams must be informed and involved in designing company vision, mission and goals and discuss freely the future action plans to act on.

It takes time to install PIE and positive relationships. It is not overnight job or it has no any quick fix formula of implementation. The process of PIE installation is critical and thus time consuming. When the management team is involved through hands-on-day-to-day participation employee involvement is easy to obtain. When employees see upper and middle management efforts, they will support and participate in them as well. A participative style allows for tapping employees inputs for decisions making processes, it provides the employees control over their jobs and encourages innovation, excellence, ownership with results and accountability for actions. The participative management process is recommended as means for encouraging teamwork and for getting results through people. PIE is not for driving employees to work harder, but about creating the conditions that will inspire them to work more effectively. The success of PIE depends critically on how effectively employees are encouraged and engaged to make their best efforts. In short, PIE is not the goal nor is it the tool, as practiced in many organizations. Rather it is a management and leadership philosophy about how people are most enabled to contribute continuous improvement that would result in an ongoing success in their work for their organization. PIE helps employees to build positive relationship between psychological empowerment and customer-oriented behavior. That is why involvement workplaces are believed to be more effective than traditional top-down management regimes.

We will talk of employee participation, involvement and empowerment all constituents of industrial democracy. Political democracy is about government, about power sharing among all the constituents of a society. We are applying for workplace democracy, so it is clear that we are talking about power sharing in the workplace and nothing less than that. Power sharing sits uneasy with the motion of managerial prerogative. Often this dilution of managerial prerogative has coincided with collective bargaining and the union power or the implementation of legislative-backed participation structures; however, there have been instances of this happening voluntarily in many organizations of the world. High performing organizations, world class management, open book management are all the heirs of industrial democracy. It is noticeable that many of the forms of participation have been aligned with various management 'fads' and the popularity of participation schemes has varied considerably over time. PIE is an integrated approach for total organizational empowerment. So first, we must look organizational empowerment through employee participation, involvement and empowerment. PIE involves distributing authority throughout the organization.

PIE FROM THE LEADER'S PERSPECTIVE

Empowering leaders behave in an empowering manner by

1. Influencing through context,
2. Creating a culture of inclusion,
3. Giving and not taking back control,
4. Providing moral and logistical support,
5. Communicating a clear mandate, and
6. Equipping people for success.

Influence through context implies trust in a higher principle or guiding force and belief in the creative potential of human nature. It is a matter of trusting the process. It is not "giving power," but creating a context where empowerment is released and nurtured. Leaders define the context and standards at every level by giving people freedom to act and innovate, thereby developing leadership and producing proactive employees, giving them a competitive edge.

Create a feeling of inclusion to nurture and empower. Develop an atmosphere of inclusion across all levels, making sure that everyone has a voice and that their voices are heard. Leaders welcome dissent as a source of objectivity and innovation. New ideas must be allowed in the decision making processes to generate solutions superior to those achieved through the exercise of positional power.

Give up control and do not reclaim it. Expect to go through a phase where managers are faced with ambiguities and a sense that things are out of control. During this uncomfortable phase, one is tempted to tighten the controls. Resist the temptation to tighten control if you want your people to use a proactive approach to problem-solving. Once responsibility is given, do not try to take it back.

Support employee empowerment. The support of superiors to their employees is critical. Fear of reprimand or sanctions by the management because an employee-made decision didn't work out will kill the efforts of the management to empower the employees. This is not delegating. Delegating is assigning a task to someone. Empowerment is the giving of responsibility and the freedom to choose the means of accomplishment. It means that the leader moves from "boss" to "coach." However, the objective must be clearly understood. Cesar Guajardo, General Director of Praxair in Mexico, wrote:

I gave people the responsibility and authority to do what they needed to improve performance. I asked them to share large-scale decisions with me. Otherwise, I gave them the authority to make decisions on their own. I encouraged small committees to share ideas and get points of view. I let common purpose, goals, and limitations. If not, employees will be hesitant. Pass the ball and let the associate run with it – but run within the ball field. Stay inbounds. Responsibility for and commitment to a clearly articulated mission is essential.

Equip people for success to insure a good chance of success. This involves training, resources, and information. Too often employees are given responsibility for which they are not equipped. This entrapment brings the feeling of being set up. Consider setting up an unallocated resource pool for solving unforeseen problems. Leaders provide their people with all the information they need by making information readily available to people at all/levels through more channels.

PIE FORM THE EMPLOYEE'S PERSPECTIVE

To experience empowerment, employees need to develop skills and practice:

1. Open communication,
2. Work in teams,
3. Critical listening,
4. Tolerance of uncertainty,
5. Resilience and courage, and
6. Accepting responsibility.

Open communication is a willingness to put our thoughts on the table; to be exposed to scrutiny; to own up to one's ideas, assumptions, biases and fears and to help others to do the same. Corporate cultures that promote creativity are characterized by direct interaction and openness-a climate where ideas are owned and challenged through honest dialogue. It may not be comfortable but it is a necessary condition of empowerment. Such openness cannot be coerced.

Willingness and know-how for working in teams is essential. It is not just self-empowerment. It is a collective change that comes by learning respect for the contributions of others. Empowerment is not a Win-Lose paradigm where an increase in the power of one results in a decrease in the power of others. In Team-Building course, participants learn to value the uniqueness of the other players. By discovering and emphasizing the gifts of each individual, the experience of empowerment increases for everyone on the team.

Gain wisdom to be fully empowered. To move from dependence on superiors for decisions, one must move beyond data, information, and knowledge to make appropriate decisions. Data is a collection of categorized numbers. Information is the meaning extracted from data. Knowledge consists of sets of information put in context, and wisdom is merging knowledge with universal principles for application to real-life situations. This requires a higher level of involvement than the old scientific management paradigm that treated employees like machines. In empowered organizations, employees across the board are committed to thinking and acting for bringing about the success of the organization, as does top management, but more effectively. Wisdom is the result of thinking about the future, recognizing trends and anticipating events or outcomes that may affect the organization and from interactions with customers, suppliers, and others with whom employees interface directly.

Tolerate uncertainty. Empowerment can be threatening. Expect some employees to resist empowerment. This is especially true when not only the outcomes, but the means and ways have always been clearly defined for them by others. Decisions about how to get things done, when left to the employee, is disquieting for the leader. This uncertainty is a change from working in an established routine where employees adhere to the rules and procedures. Under pressure, employees tend to run to the leader seeking resolution and closure. Leaders who do not understand the dynamics of empowerment, out of misdirected compassion or because it makes them feel more powerful, often succumb to these requests by telling them what to do. This is disempowering and reestablishes dependence. If employees are encouraged to think for themselves, goals and boundaries need to be clearly defined. This establishes guidelines for use of intuition and thinking across departments and disciplines for solutions related to their common purpose.

Resilience and courage come from within. The source of confidence is not in others but in one's own inner strength. Empowerment means to be forward thinking enough to live with mistakes and failures without being desired results. This enables them to learn from their mistakes. Empowered employees are willing to have their performance measured by objective written assessments because these are opportunities for feedback and improvement. Part of responsibility happens when you see inappropriate management conduct or receive inappropriate direction. It is important to document all incidents and save them in a safe place.

PIE FROM THE ORGANIZATION'S PERSPECTIVE

Empowerment calls for organizations to

1. be more decentralized,
2. share more information,
3. have in place a system of contingent rewards,
4. be team-based, and
5. align itself with its goals and values.

Decentralization distributes decision-making as close to the action as appropriate. This means giving employees the authority to make timely decisions, Individual empowerment cannot occur within a highly centralized system of control because such systems reserve decision-making power for the few who occupy the center, thus inhibiting individual initiative. People are not motivated to change when they don't have authority to do anything with what they have learned.

Information sharing is empowering. Hoarding knowledge and withholding it is a way to maintain control. Employees need information about the organization's mission and goals, information needed to meet team objectives, and information about their individual performance. In empowering organizations, information is no longer the property of individuals, but now belongs to the entire group. As information is more openly shared, the organization will begin to function less on the basis of opinion and bias and more on the basis of facts. Systems must be in place to enable access to both general information about the organization and also specific information about the performance of their particular department or team.

Contingent rewards are difficult to design. Empowerment works best when a reward system distinguishes between employees based on performance. Empowering organizations reward employees who make decisions that contribute to the accomplishment of the organization's purpose and goals. Make sure that what is rewarded reflects goals of the organization. To automatically punish failure inhibits empowerment. It is better to reward employees for attempting new ideas, even ones that fail. Paige Leavitt, of the American Productivity and Quality Center in Houston, explains how they use rewards to encourage empowerment:

"We try to foster an atmosphere that has a lot of respect for people who make a contribution. We don't expect success every time a person suggests or tries something, otherwise they won't want to try new things. If you've come up with a good idea and your supervisor sends you a thank-you note or gives you a pat on the back – that does more than anything that we can do in an employee newsletter or a public venue. [Schweitzer, C. (2004) Light-bulb leadership: Creating a culture where innovation is in. (Association Management 56(8), 31–42.)

Teams develop when individuals move outside themselves and become concerned with the success of all other members. This means that employees become concerned, not only with the success of their immediate responsibility, but also with success of the other members of the team. Then the group becomes a unit where the development of one member increases the power of the team.

Alignment with the common purpose is a must. To empower people in an unaligned organization can be counterproductive. If people do not share a common vision, and do not share common goals, empowering people will increase organizational stress and make it impossible to maintain coherence and direction. An organizational commitment to empowerment would be foolish if leaders did not share the same visions and goals. Empowered organizations must structure processes, goals, people, and reward systems aligned with each other.

The construct of PIE need to be part of long term strategy of the organization. PIE initiatives should be guided by the dual objectives of improving organizational effectiveness and improving the quality of work life for employees. Too often, PIE interventions have been viewed on simple way to motivate employees to do more. Ethical issues and long term effects on employees must become part of the landscape for PIE efforts at present and in future. Therefore organization/management must keep some promises:

- ❖ that management must involve employees in the decisions that will ultimately affect them, as employees will have more interest in getting involved in matters of importance to them personally.
- ❖ that management need to take into consideration the individual differences in the employees in their work group, an variability in ability and motivation will impact participation and involvement
- ❖ that management provide access to relevant information and resources will contribute to the likelihood of successful involvement.
- ❖ that management removing unnecessary bureaucratic controls and constraints will ease successful completion of tasks.
- ❖ that the management must facilitate flexibility, learning and participation, fair and constructive judgment of ideas, rewards and recognitions, mechanisms of developing new ideas, an active flow of new ideas, and a shared vision. Leaders should act as role models, set appropriate goals with employees, involvement to ensure suitable empowerment to work groups, value individual contributions and to show confidence in employees.

Thus PIE efforts will be successful and the facilitating conditions in which employees will actually experience involvement at work. In short for psychological, social, economic PIE, four factors of job and job place are having positive orientation to the employee work role. Those are

- ❖ meaningfulness – the value of the task goal or purpose,
- ❖ competence – self efficacy or personal mastery; it is individual belief in his capabilities and skills.
- ❖ Choice – a strong internal locus or control –
- ❖ Self management and self determination, and impact – the degree to which participative behavior is seen as making difference in terms of accomplishing the purpose of the task.

Impact builds on the concept locus of control and the belief that one has an influence on the organization's level of decision-making policy. This characterizes the impact and the degree to which an employee can influence strategic, managerial, administrative and operating outcomes at work.

PIE – DIFFERENCE IN MEANING

In people management, the terms participation, involvement and empowerment (PIE) are frequently used within the literature but often interpreted quite differently depending on the perspective of leader/author. Therefore, first it is necessary to distinguish between participation and involvement and then examine where empowerment fits within these perspectives. According to Chartered Institute of Personal Management (CIPD):

Employee participation is defined as a process of employee involvement designed to provide employee with the opportunity to influence and where appropriate take part in decision making on matters which affect them

Employee involvement is a range of processes designed to engage the support, understanding and optimum contribution of all employees in an organization and their commitment to its objectives.

Employee Empowerment entails some additional employee choice at the margins of their jobs rather than any substantial increase in employee choice.

The difference between employee participation and employee involvement are twofold, while employee participation fosters a team approach and work is completed by group of co-employees sharing the same goal, the employee involvement links the employee with a different connection to management. This allows employees in the involvement approach to offer ideas regarding the work until a decision is reached. Both approaches can foster a strong sense of commitment to the common goal. But the benefits of employee involvement and employee empowerment are there if employee participation is implemented effectively.

Employee participation – When an employee participates in a business activity, it means he shares the activity with others. These others form one team and the employee is responsible for the completion of a goal. The team provides the forum where the employee can suggest ideas to make the items more efficiently and can contribute to decisions from his position on the team's project. Whether the level of the employee's involvement is major or minor; all members are encouraged to participate.

Employee involvement involves a one-to-one approach between the employee and management. This is more direct method of handling a work project, as the individual employee is involved in all aspects of the decisions making process. This process encourages an employee to take ownership of the outcome of the project. The employees affect the processes by making decisions with the management, and this encourages the employees to become more involved in the project and to share their ideas as to how to improve their projects. Employees' involvement is the process through which people change the working structure of an organization in order to develop a new way of working. It shares many of the features of the participation processes but it is usually more involved and takes place over a longer period of time. It is often used when an organization needs to change the way it does something. The key to involvement is that the people being involved become active stakeholders with ownership of the eventual outcome. Consequently, if an organization is committed to employees' involvement then, as Holden postulates, a number of factors will need addressing for the proper implementation of employees' involvement systems:

- ❖ a willingness by the management to concede some of their prerogatives.
- ❖ the necessity to train managers in employee involvement initiatives.
- ❖ to have a clear policy regarding the role and prerogatives of line managers in relation to senior management and the workforce under their supervision.
- ❖ the necessity to train workers in group working skills such as presentation, leadership, assertiveness, problem solving etc.

- ❖ the necessity of providing proper feedback mechanisms which clearly indicate the workforce is being listened to and not purely lip service fashion.
- ❖ the action is being taken to implement group decisions. This reinforces the news amongst the workforce that their contributions are well received.
- ❖ that conflicting views have a place in developing initiatives.

Employee participation is also a process in which employees are involved in the decision making. They are involved when they are given authority or empowerment.

Employee empowerment is a method that involves passing down the authority to perform tasks to workers. Employee empowerment goes further way, by allowing employees some degree of control over how the task should be undertaken. This is called delegation of powers. Delegation involves passing down of authority to perform tasks and take decisions from higher to lower levels of organization. It should be remembered that it is only the task that is assigned to the subordinate but the final responsibility rests in the hands of the manager. So employee empowerment is the involvement of employee after they are given delegated powers.

Where as employee involvement means that every employee is unique in nature and each employee means a lot to the company. It also refers that every employee is important for the success of business as they are working hard to achieve the goals that are set by the organization. Each employee's inputs is valued and respected by the management of the company and each employee is involved in the day-to-day running of business. Employees' involvement is something that makes the employees feel that they are worth a lot to the company and the company really needs them; this eventually results in the employees being highly motivated.

Chapter 9
WISDOM OF TEAMS

- ❖ Merits of Decentralization
- ❖ Small Is Beautiful (Teams)
- ❖ Team Working
- ❖ Types of Teams

Chapter 9
WISDOM OF TEAMS

MERITS OF DECENTRALIZATION

A. Centralization VS Decentralization

Liberalization, privatization, globalization and open boundary less market are the new horizons where to days industrial houses have to fight battles for business survival. But this' situation-oriented awareness' is missing among many traditional organizations. It is because they believe in centralization of business activities and managing big organizations in a centralized manner. As a result:

- ❖ The centralizer (leader) harbor an auto-pilot mind set and his means of trying to run every business activity from the top with minimal participation and involvement of rank and file. This evidence shows that centralization and its trapping have been a great drag on quality management, quality of work life, productivity, efficiency and human relations at work. The centralized "big" approach stifles rather than fostering the very basic of "organizing small:" quality circles, work improvement teams, task force, project teams etc.
- ❖ Organizational leaders work on the assumption that the spirit and motivation of the employees will be unaffected by the structural measures taken to comply with centralism precepts. Structure that states their roles, responsibilities and feeling of fulfillment.
- ❖ This centralism has exacted a heavy toll in employee apathy, which creates lack-luster performance management and employees

generally not communicate well in day-to-day issues. Centralization breeds and nurtures managership and not leadership.

❖ Those superficial changes do little to create the initiative, innovation and ingenuity that come through only humanistic practices.

❖ Centralism style, traditional management role and their practices are messy, contradictory and often thorny business of affecting employees belief about their work, work place, their managers and there in outcome.

In a nutshell, the traditional management approach of some past organizations and even some of those today can be considered as the major culprit in the improvement of an organization. Today's globalization of business and open market economies has exposed the inadequacies of traditional management and that their learning disabilities were hidden for a long time. These were not visible or easy to spot before because local comparisons were coloured by identical cultural influences. Traditional management was born of a die-hard culture that was developed much earlier and which made organizations to become unaware of strong outside competitions, thereby preventing them from forced introspections and effective changes. In short, traditional management kept the economic status of the organization insulated till date. But those days are gone now. The new people management has taken root. Now the alternative approach towards managing business is "organizing small" work groups. All possible obstructive functional walls have been broken down, complex functions have been dissected to be managed by small effective teams and employee involvement and empowerment have been established and encouraged to release the awesome power of the human spirit and its corresponding resources. The present management practices are the new realities. Borderless market places, discriminating customers, global democratic diversities, and the appeal for maximum customer delight, both internal as well as external, are the new and prevailing mantras of the liberalized and global organizations. Those who were unmoved by appeals to select home-built products and services for patriotic reasons, are now taking the highest care of their customers for best value additions, quality products and services, quality of work and the balance of work and home life. Therefore, the felt need is very clear. Every organizational element can be changed substantially and even drastically improved. However, the extent of success in each case depends on the management's willingness and commitment to abandon unwanted traditional management approaches for the new and better ways. The style of closed management system, the organizational behavior, attitude and total mental revolution is to adopt from organizing small team with due participation and empowerment.

"SMALL IS BEAUTIFUL"

You can't have leadership in every field unless you believe in it. Bottom-up approach is only possible when people are given true participation, involvement and empowerment to manage their work activities. Managing small work groups are particularly good at combining talents and providing innovative solutions to possible unfamiliar problems in cases where there is no well established approach or procedure. The wider skill and knowledge set of the group has a distinct advantage over that of the individual. In general, however, there are overriding advantages in a group-based work force which makes it attractive to the management because it engenders a fuller utilization of the work-force. A small group can be seen as a self-managing unit. The range of skills provided by its members are self-monitoring where each group performs its given task, thereby making it a reasonably safe recipient for the delegation of authority and responsibility, even if the problems could be decided by a single person. There are two main benefits that involve the people who will carry out the decision. Firstly, the motivational aspect of participation by the employees in the involvement of decision-making, followed by their empowerment which will clearly enhance its implementation. Secondly, there may well be factors which the implementer understands better than the single person (leader) who could supposedly have decided alone. More indirectly, if each of the lowest echelons of the work force became trained through participation in group decision-making, in the context and understanding of the company's objectives and work practices, then each will be better able to solve work-related problems in general. Further, they will also individually become a safe recipient for delegated authority. Again from the individual's point of view, there is added incentive that through belonging to a group each can participate in achievements well beyond his own individual potential less idealistically, the group provides an environment where the individuals self-perceived level of responsibility and authority is enhanced, in environment where the individuals self-perceived level of responsibility and authority is enhanced, in an environment where accountability is shared, thus providing a perfect motivator through enhanced self-esteem coupled with low stress. Finally, a word about much "wanted" recognition of the worth of the individual, which is often given as the reason for delegating authority to group subordinates. The bottom line is that the individual's talents are better utilized in a group and not because they are wonderful human beings. Finally, the human factor is crucial to the success in the management of small group.

TEAM WORKING

It is thus a collaborative management intervention through which management design organizational changes and carry it out in policies, procedures, methods, structures and so on. Team working puts a fundamental organizational development programme going. The reality is that much of the organizations work is accomplished directly or indirectly through teams. Work teams culture exerts a significant influence on individual behavior. A team is a form of group, but has characteristics in greater degree than ordinary groups, including higher commitment to common goals and a higher degree of interdependency and interaction. When such teams engage in problem solving activities directed toward task accomplishment, the team members build something together and it appears the act of building something together also builds a sense of camardship, cohesion and spirit decrops. The underlying assumption regarding teams in organizations is that resources are available in the individuals in the work unit. They have the capability to address and deal with the questions, if given the time, encouragement and freedom needed to work honestly toward solutions. Teams formation and their development in its best sense is crafting the opportunity for people to come together to share their concerns, their ideas and their experiences and to begin to work together to solve their mutual problems and achieve common goals. The basic building blocks of organizations are teams and one of the basic building blocks of organization development is team building(William Dyres-Team Building: issues and Alternatives).

TEAM BUILDING

It breeds and nurtures leadership and each depend on each other. You need leadership to be successful, but you won't have it unless you empower people to exercise it. Therefore, team building requires following few issues to be address prominently.

❖ **Decentralize the organization** – The decentralization approach affects every aspect of management, systems operation and interactions not only the structure, but also all facets of organizational character, culture and climate. It takes the human spirit and the human system aspects into full account. Small groups, all the time, put the health and goals of the organization above everything else.

❖ **Create leaders not managers** – Leaders think of involvement, empower others to make decisions. He think of dynamic, caring human system, improving initiative and innovation. They (leaders) shape organizations character, create more leaders to lead the organization ahead. Because they understand opinions, feelings by getting actual facts out for everyone's benefits.

❖ **Recognize People, People and People** – Techniques, technologies and development produce quality or excellence in the work people do. The qualitative excellence of an organization comes from the people who believe that anything and everything can be done in a much better way. What people need is liberation so as to be involved and empowered in order to reach their fullest potential. It is human relations that is important and you can build human relations only if you are in touch with the people.

❖ **Create ownership at their level** – People who are part of the team' own' the company and 'own' their jobs. Regularly perform a thousand percent better than they are involved. You don't have to define responsibility, you always assumed and share. Ownership demands the enhancement of pride, pride in ourselves and our close associates. Ownership means being involved in a business. Turn ownership on people. They will turnout organization positively. JRD Tata once said "aim high but go into details." And details I mean give participation through empowering people.

WISDOM OF TEAMS

Managing small working and result oriented groups, I called them 'small is beautiful.' These groups/teams undertake various work improvement projects. They plan and do the projects themselves; they also check and evaluate the project and implement relevant solutions through problem solving techniques. The teams and their members, possessing complementary abilities, skills, knowledge and a host of other competencies are committed to the common performance goals of the project as well as in developing healthy work relationships for which they hold themselves mutually accountable. The heart of any team is a shared commitment by its members for their performance. There are, indeed, many types of teams operating in various kinds of organizations. They are empowered to take own decisions to solve the problems on the spot. They use quality tools, brain storming, nominal group techniques and other methods to investigate a given problem and to find collective solutions at their end. They present their success stories to the management with details of cost-saving, additional revenue generation, improved work methods, workplaces and work conditions. Their involvement with empowerment gives them extreme satisfaction and inculcates a feeling of ownership with organization as a whole. This prudential performance of groups/teams is transferred enough to reflect vision being translated into success, consistently. It is observed that following types of teams are more effective at work as empowered teams.

TYPES OF TEAMS

1. **Problem Solving Teams** – It focuses on specific issues in their areas of responsibility, develop potential solutions and are often empowered to take action within defined limits. Their members usually are employees from a specific department who met at least once in a week. Teams may have authority to implement their own solutions if they don't require major procedural changes that might adversely affect other operations or require substantial new resources. Managers delegate certain problems and decision making responsibilities to a team. In brief the team problem solving is likely to be supervisor to individual problem solving.

    ❖ The greater the diversity of information, experience and approaches to be found in a team, the greater is the importance to the task at hand.

    ❖ Acceptance of decisions arrived at is crucial for effective implementation by team members.

    ❖ Participation is important for reinforcing the values of representation versus authoritanism and demonstrating respect for individual members through team processes and

    ❖ Team members rely on each other in performing their jobs.

2. **Self-Managed Teams** – These teams normally consists of employees who must work together effectively and daily to manufacture or provide an entire service to customers. A major characteristic of such teams is that they are empowered with discretion and are therefore effective to perform important and valuable tasks in an atmosphere of independence. This allows them to experience a sense of importance and significance (impact) in the work performed and the goals achieved. They can be workable in any area of organization. These teams typically eliminate one or more managerial levels thereby creating a flatter organization. Empowered self-managed teams are not necessarily right for every organization or every situation.

3. **Cross-Functional Teams** – These teams bring together persons from different functions to work on a common task. Cross-Functional Teams draw members from various Functional teams operate on an extended basis and these are disbanded after the problems that have addressed have been solved and the goals achieved. Such teams are often useful in situations that require innovations, speed, cost-cutting, deliveries and focus in responding to customer needs. These teams are best used in the sales and marketing areas, particularly in the area of retail customers.

4. **Virtual Teams** – Functional problem solving, cross functional and even self-managed teams can increasingly operate as virtual teams. A virtual team is a group of individuals who collaborate through various information technologies. Unlike teams that operate primarily through person-to-person meetings by members of the same organization, virtual team work primarily across distance or any place, anytime and increasingly a cross organizational boundaries from two or more organizations. Clear, concise and mutually agreed upon goals are the glue that holds virtual team together. Everyone in a virtual team needs to be autonomous and self-reliant while simultaneously working collaboratively with others. The duality requires a certain type of person and a foundation of trust among team members. The most apparent feature of a virtual team is the array of technology based links used to connect members and enable them to carry out its tasks. Virtual teams are increasingly common because of rapid advances in computer and telecommunication technologies. Such teams are effective in surveys, having a wide range of operations like product customer networks and opinion polls. Different software systems, inter-net and intra-net are the main enabler of virtual teams. They allow virtual teams to access text, visual, audio and numerical data in a user friendly manner. The internet and intra-net also allow virtual teams to compile the contacts of organizational members and important stake-holders, such as suppliers as well as intimating customer updates on a team's progress.

5. **Quality Circle Teams** – It is a team used for problem solving in the organization. It consists of seven to ten members from a department or across the department, who volunteered to meet together regularly to analyze and make project proposals about product quality cost reduction, waste elimination, safety and such other problems. Recommendations are forwarded to steering committee. Leaders are encouraged to create a high degree of participation within the team. The use of quality circles has been one of the central aspects in the evolution of TQM a much broader strategy, like quality circle teams; kaizan team, Five 5 teams, project teams, task force etc. are the teams working in organizations for find out solutions to the problems. Particularly through these all teams employee participation, involvement and their empowerment is visible in today organizations.

A fundamental belief in organizations of today is that work teams are building blocks of organizational development and its success, And teams and team work are the part of the foundations of organizational development Effective teams produce results for beyond the performance of unrelated individuals. Teams are important for number of reasons.

i. Much individual behavior is rooted in the socio-cultural norms and values of the work team. If the team, changes these norms and values the effect on individual behavior are immediate and lasting.

ii. Many tasks are so complex and they can't be performed by single individual. People must work together to accomplish them.

iii. Teams create synergy that is the sum of the efforts of team members is far greater than the sum of individual efforts or people working alone. Synergy is a principal reason teams are so important.

iv. Teams satisfy people's needs for social interaction, status recognition and respect. Teams nurture human nature.

Top peters assert in "liberation management" book that cross functional autonomous and empowered teams are what the best organizations are using right now to out distance the competition. High responsibility, clear objectives and high accountability drive project teams to outperform traditional organization structure on every measurable dimension. Teams have always been an important foundation for organizational development, but there is growing awareness of the team's unique ability to create synergy, respond quickly and flexibly to problems, find new way to get job done and satisfy social needs in the workplace. Peter continues to advocate employee participation and empowerment stating that today's jobs are best accomplished through empowered people working in highly autonomous teams and advised that the organizations must be redesigned to allow that to happen. Empowerment to employees is an important ingredient in high performing organizations of today.

Chapter 10

PIE INTERVENTIONS

Chapter 10
PIE INTERVENTIONS

WHAT WE MEAN BY INTERVENTIONS?

Interventions focus on initiatives deemed appropriate for the enhancement or development of an organization. Organizational interventions are initiatives that have proved its effectiveness in creating positive changes within organizations. It has been experienced that through interventions one can bring about changes in management which would enliven the organizations thereby creating important enablers for work improvements. Interventions are the guidelines to provide an overview of the organizational renewal, partially or fully, depending upon the interventions initiated. Interventions can help to address and to mitigate the burden of employers as well as employees. Action research through interventions is ideally suited to provide actionable knowledge derived from collaborative work on various organizational issues. It provides relevant, rich and reflective information gathered as processes and changes occur. Action research projects methods often used are both qualitative and quantitative and can provide both theoretical and practical insight into the subject. Secondly, intervention presentations and its implementations address some aspects of building relational ties between management and employees, individuals and work groups and ties between members in different (cross groups) functional areas.

WHY INTERVENTIONS ARE NEEDED?

The concepts of employee participation, involvement and empowerment (PIE) are embedded into two ideological groups and each one imparts to the ideas, its assumptions, perceptions, judgments and reflections on its implementation and practices. The first group is organizational psychology and the other is political economy. The first group can fairly be said to take a psychological social approach. From their perspectives employees PIE is intended to reduce the mental anguish, emotional disturbances and existential angust that employees experience when;

- ❖ They believe that they are treated with less respect than they deserve.
- ❖ They are denied consideration on individuals.
- ❖ When their experiences is discounted.
- ❖ They have 'no say' in their work routine.
- ❖ They are supervised by immature boss who do not recognize their values as contributors to a common project.

Employees in such situation tend to be resentful, unmotivated and unproductive. To modify these attitudes and behaviors PIE promotes shared responsibility between manager and managed creating a working community with a positive organizational culture. Interventions like PIE are the advanced means to enhance the quality of employee's collective efficiency in the workplace. Employees who are highly esteemed will be happy and proud of their work. The creation of a competent and perhaps even enthusiastic organization depends on both its leadership and its subordinate employees, both of which pursue work efficiency. In order to achieve this, PIE incorporates a works culture that is compatible to PIE.

The other group that is focused on 'political economy' is characterized by relationships that dominate and control the employees (command and control). Individual satisfactions and frustrations alike are deemed to be the products of structural relationships. Their mediation of wage theory calls for industrial democracy authoritarianship. (Raman Vera) They are only concerned with their power and authority. The assumptions of the political economy characterized by command and control, often leads to the acknowledgement of unavoidable friction and management conflicts between groups, whereas the first group pays attention to human relations, individual personality and motivation (PIE Interventions | 141). Secondly, attention is focus on collaboration, cooperation and collective bargaining. No doubt the approaches of both groups are mainly intended to keep organizations working, but the range of options under the first group of employees are impressive:

❖ The right of employees to meaningful participation in workplace decision making about industrial matters.
❖ The right of employees to be consulted before decisions that will significantly affect their employment are implemented.
❖ Encouragement of employees share ownership programs
❖ Assistance for the development of cooperative activities.
❖ To ensure that they are empowered and involved in solving problems related to work and workplace.

Over the decades a number of organizational strategies, initiatives and interventions have been applied to work situations only through employee PIE in order to maximize productivity and performance. It was largely recognized especially in large public and private sectors that employees frustration and disappointment have measurable production costs in terms of personality disorders: frustration, de-motivation, job dissatisfaction, low morale etc. The awareness and cure of this is to initiate team working through PIE in order to build team spirit and the feeling of togetherness with a positive frame of mind, thereby activating employees toward performance, action and achievement. Ask and listen, instead of providing your (Manager's) thought, ask employees of business issues problem solutions and when it comes from (manager's) They:

❖ Delegate opportunity to someone passionate about the issues.
❖ Identify champions within the business, to lead and implement the change.
❖ You empower employee who is making difference to the business.

Their involvement creates a win-win situation; you win by delegating, the business wins by improving processes and performance and most importantly the employees feel like primary winners because they have the opportunity to implement their own ideas to an issue and bring about resolution. Suggestion system, quality circles, kaizen teams, 5 'S' teams, task force teams, self managed teams, are the interventions to invite employee involvement by undertaking 'do it yourself' problem solving projects.

WHY ORGANIZATIONAL RENEWAL?

Organizations will only improve as the people who work there improve their practices. Much of what we currently do in terms of people development is isolated, rarely ever changing and rarely related to organizational goals. Effective professional and personal development occurs at the inter-section of meeting both organizational needs and individual needs. How does it typically happen in your organization? For every failure, there is an alternative course of action. You need to find it. The primary responsibility of a business leader is to remove roadblocks so that people can innovate, participate and move organization's mission forward. Change is a difficult process without roadblocks in the way. So what is preventing the necessary changes that need to take place? How are you contributing to these road blocks as a leader? What road blocks can you move out of the way for your stake holder is the prime duty and responsibility of the leader. All that is available in human society depends upon the opportunities for development accorded to individuals.

"Organizations are like kids, it is all about development. If you serve them with good, strong values, a clear vision of the future and the view that everything is possible, they will grow up to be like that and vice versa." (Zal Kind)

You just have to it. It is a kind of good grooming. People don't want to know the details but you have to got to look and smell good as you walk out on shop floor/office.

Organizational change interventions represent the perspectives and lessons learned of a number of leaders (organization), who have been engaged in organizational development work over a long term. These individuals are continuing to learn more about what it takes to be an effective organization and the role that organizational development plays in achieving organizational mission. The process of learning is continuous, what are the successive ways of organizational development work and how do organization continue to develop in an intentional way? How do you integrate organizational development and change management programs work, so that they are mutually reinforcing. How can those organization, which have experienced the positive impact on organizational development work on their mission and objectives and how work is articulated that is having connection in a way that is compelling to other organization. How employees of the organization do experienced the impact of organizational development work. All these questions and many more are programs implementable under organizational development.

Significant organizational changes occur when an organization changes its overall strategy for success, adds or removes a major section or practice and or wants to change the very nature by which it operates. It also occurs when an organization evolves through various life cycles just like people must evolve through their life cycle. For organizations to develop, they often must undergo significant changes at various points in their development. Why is there a need for organizational improvement and what solutions are available? PIE approach is supposed to be the path finder. PIE paves the way through these pavers: POSITIVE HUMAN RELATIONS; PARTICIPATION; INVOLVEMENT AND EMPOWERMENT. However, majority of organization leaders are unaware of it or pretend to be unaware, although there have been a history of some such approaches as we have seen under organizational psychology and political economy (command and control) (power and authority).

WHY CHANGE IS INVITABLE?

Change management can be a powerful organizational development intervention whether by building critical communication skills, instilling core company values or teaching strategic thinking. Change can make a significant impact on an organization's success as a whole if they are designed and delivered with care. There are number of reasons why organizations implemented these interventions ranging from improving employee participation to improve performance-quality of work and work life, management reengineering, renewal of management practices; knowledge management, employee and organization learning for development, so that significant value addition to organizations is made visible. An organization's ability to stay competitive in today's knowledge economy is because organizational factors help contribute to the change processes that need to be carried out. These include such factors such as organization support, commitment, employee involvement, commitments to get involved in designing and delivery of such initiatives. These changes that are brought about through management interventions with employees maximize the organization's chances of improving and enhancing organizational effectiveness. Interventions are broadly defined as building bridges between current and potential performances, organizational capabilities and the creative abilities of the employees. The values of developing employee participation and involvement have been recognized as the starting point of it.

The question is not merely one of setting up development interventions or initiatives and selecting the relevant ones to be stressed for implementation, but rather in seeing that these interventions as one of the dynamic systems within the organizational systems in coping up with the organization's inter-connectedness in an appropriate manner. Generally, common sets of organizational improvements and competencies pertaining to employees and their organizations are:

- ❖ Management of organizational change and development, adaption to changing situation.
- ❖ Promoting continuous learning and development.
- ❖ Participating, involving and empowering employees in organizational problem solving processes.
- ❖ Introducing and extending quality management principles and practices at work.
- ❖ Managing cultural change and diversity issues.
- ❖ Clear two-way communication.
- ❖ Building leadership and relational skills.

It is important for an organization to create an atmosphere where employees can experiment with new skills, new knowledge and behavior that they learnt. Given all the contributing factors, organizational leaders if wish to implement all such interventions step by step, it will start making sure that there is full organizational support. The leader will do an organizational readiness assessment to make certain that the senior management will feel a sense of urgency as regards the ideas of organizational development as well as understanding its implications and possibilities, thereafter giving all the necessary backing to carry out necessary developments in the organization. This would set the stage by ensuring that the organization has the right environment to support its as well as the individuals' successes.

If any organization is looking to implement these interventions that are truly valuable to their employees and to their businesses, it is then critical that the organizational leader remains open to revaluating and changing the nature of the interventions in order to ensure that it stays as relevant and useful as is possible. The best leader/manager will understand that his organizational success depends not on his or his management's own technical and financial abilities but rather on the abilities of those who work with them. Secondly, organizational change should not be conducted for the sake of change. Organizational change efforts should be geared to improve the performance of organizations. Therefore, it is useful to have some understanding of what is meant by organizational performance. It is employee groups and organizational practices demonstrating performance in integrated efforts.

There are a number of very useful tools to help leaders to effectively explore, understand and communicate the needs of their organizations as well as to guide successful changes in their organizations. At the same time, there are different types of organizational changes, including planned versus unplanned changes, which are organizational-wide versus changes that are primarily relevant to just one part of the organization. These changes can be incremental, meaning that they may be slow and gradual on the one hand and radical or fundamental on the other hand. Knowing which types of changes you are doing will help people to retain the scope and perspective during the many complexities that presently cause enormous frustrations during such changes.

These are some of the tested, well organized organizational development change models from which to manage change effort. Interventions such as Organizational Behavior (OB), Organizational Development (OD), Organizational & Individual Learning (OIL), Knowledge Management (KM), Management Reengineering (MR), Total Quality Management (TQM), Six-sigma (SS), Performance Management Measurement & Development (PMMD), Total Operating Performance (TOP), or Management By Objectives (MBO) are some of the major interventions carried out by various organizations in the world. They are from manufacturing, service, hospitality, education, health care, Tourism, commercial and service sectors.

It must be kept in mind that there is no consensus on a workable set of principles in any given organizational change; relevant learning and applications are rooted in deeply held assumptions and values. This means that it is useful to make values that underlie a different approach to change and explicit learning as well as to subjects that call for of discussions.

ORGANIZATIONAL CHANGE PERSEPECTIVES

There are multiple perspectives on change and organizing organizational change.

- ❖ Basic Values in organizing are s strong belief in human potential, participation in workplace and interpersonal relationship based on trust and openness.
- ❖ Basic Values in changing are employee participation, involvement in the change process and learning through feedback and collective reflection by all actors.
- ❖ Human beings are seen on being inherently good, creative and searching for new experiences to develop their human potential.
- ❖ Human beings are open, purposeful people who use conversation in preparation of concerted action and constructing realities.

- ❖ Organizations are seen as purposeful social and technical systems in interaction with each other.
- ❖ Organizations are seen as open systems in interaction with environment.
- ❖ Change is aimed at enabling organizations to be effective in their relations with their environment and to contribute to the quality of work life.
- ❖ Change is treated not as discrete events but as a process with phases and logical flows.
- ❖ Change practices and interventions are based on the application of behavioral sciences.
- ❖ Change practices relay on knowledge about individuals and their relationships in organizations.
- ❖ Learning is collective, ongoing and cognitive activity of all participants in change and fueled by experimentation in and reflection on practices and methodologies.
- ❖ A key issue to organizational development and change is to integrate the interests and needs of individuals with the collective interest of organizations.

When organizing, changing and learning are seen as interactive processes in which people construct their relationships, activities and meanings, the basic assumptions and methodology of organizational change are constructed in a new way. This way of looking at organizational change might be helpful in understanding the tensions between organizational development and planned change, it provides ways to understand our own bias and dilemmas of organizing and change and helps to choose a position between the two sides of the dilemmas.

Finally, it is to say that organizations do not exist by themselves in a vacuum but are part of interactive and dynamic environments. In today's highly turbulent landscape of extremely competitive environments in such areas as communications, and technology, developments, changes in laws and liberalization, privatization and globalization (LPG), the modern organizations face considerable pressure to meet or exceed customers and stakeholders expectations by delivering products and services that are of the highest quality. And it is clear that what is needed to survive into this millennium is the ability of the organization to respond and adopt. This will require visionary leadership and a change-oriented mind-set. The key to establishing an effective change and organizational transformation of organization lies in assessing and diagnosing present situation and then start change management interventions. "All successful innovations, including human factors, interventions needs to address the problems of organizational inertia as well as active opposition and resistance."

– (Balton and Heap)

Chapter 11

PIE INTERVENTIONS IN ACTION

I.   Turn Around Management (TAM)

II.   Organizational Behavior (OB)

III. Organization Development (OD)

IV. Individual and Organizational (I & O)

V.   Knowledge Management (KM)

VI. Total Quality Management (TQM)

VII. Business Process Reengineering (BPR)

PIE:-   P – Participation

        I – Involvement

       E – Empowerment

Chapter 11
PIE INTERVENTIONS IN ACTION

I.   TURN AROUND MANAGEMENT (TAM)

The Change Management Strategy

Basically the employee does not have a responsibility to manage any organizational change. Responsibility for managing is with organization leader and his management team. They must manage the change in a way that employee can cope with it. The management has the responsibility to facilitate and enable change. Changes such as new management structure, systems, styles, human resources policies, total performance management, business expansion, collaboration, merger, relocation, financial or strategic business units (SBU), structuring or reengineering of management by downsizing, right sizing, delayering, reducing the size of firm in terms of number of employees, divisions units and hierarchal levels in the organization or process management, process innovation or process redesigning, work flow or adding new departments such as MIS, ERP, SAP etc. for the purpose of improving cost, quality, service, speed and people management, to improve total operating performance (TOP) of the organization. All such changes we termed as turnaround management strategies. Turnaround management (TAM) is the strategic management process does not end when the organization decides with strategy or strategies to pursue. There must be a translation of strategic thought into strategic action. This translation is much easier if the management and employees of the organization understand the business and feel a part of the organization through involvement in strategy and formulation activities.

Without participation, involvement and commitment of employees, such strategy implementation efforts face major problems of failures.

Human Side of Change Process

Turnaround management initiatives create new systems and environments which need to be explained to employees as early as possible, so that employee's involvement in validating and redefining the changes themselves can be obtained. Please keep in mind that whenever an organization imposes new things on employees there will be difficulties. Participation, involvement and open early full communication are the important factors to accept new changes. In short, you can't impose change. People and teams need to be empowered to find their own solutions and responses, but with the facilitation and support from leaders and managers in a context of tolerance and compassion. Management and leadership styles and behaviours are more important than clever processes and policies. Employees need to be able to trust the organization.

Turnaround management or organizational change is about people changing. Organizational change then is a highly complex process that must take into account how employees respond psychologically when asked to make major changes at work. Their reaction may invariably vary. Some will be supportive, others will be reactive. Therefore, human side of change must be frequently handled with adequate care. "The rule of change, therefore, is to begin any process change with concern for its impact on employees. The second rule is to prepare employees for the change by educating them in what they need to know in order for the change to be successful, the third rule is to involve them in the change as much as is possible in the change that is to take place, and the fourth rule concerns their involvement with the change as to what really needs to be changed about the entire system in order for the efforts to produce real results." (W.A. Parmore, creating strategic change).

Organizations are dynamic systems and like all other systems, they do not function when their components do not work together smoothly and efficiently. Any change we introduce to organization must be aligned with an ever changing, dynamic and culturally diverse workplace. Understanding the relationship between turn around and management and employees in the key to improving your organization's ability to move through change effectively. Turn around management often means making critical decision about how to deploy or re-deploy human resources. Knowing the goals and objectives of each individual in the organization can be difficult task. Solutions can provide you with the means to easily align the goals of your employees to the overall mission of the organization will help to develop an effective solution for turnaround management by accessing the workforce mind and their alignment to the issues of change. Turn around management promises fundamental changes as a result of organizational renewal. It is therefore, of direct concern personally, professionally and economically to all those working in the organization. In nutshell, change requires participation of people who must themselves change for organizational transformation to succeed.

It is experienced that even today many organization hired employees to work for so the organization choose them, judge them and reward them for their ability to perform specific task. This is not workable solution in today organizations. Today's organizations hire people to work with, as a part of community of shared aspirations, ideals and trust. The ability to perform a specific task is not enough; today organizations need people who add value to every process they touch and who bring values to the organization. The management of choosing, judging and rewarding have to be change to the understand the turnaround management change effect. Each process must be quality tool in its own right. Modern organizations depend on high performing employees working together in a safe and healthy workplace where diversity, development and team work are valued and recognized. We take care of the employees' products which they will create and from which profit will follow. By taking care of the employees they, in turn, will deliver the impeccable services demanded by customers, both internal and external. The logic of the new time's revolutionary times is a people-focused management.

People must know that their ideas will be listened to and if they have merit, acted upon. If they do, it is possible to mobilize industrial creativity on a very broad scale. We therefore, must mobilize enable and communicate employees. Again it is not enough to get people mobilized, energized. You have to give them the wherewithal and that requires enabling, redesigning work practices so that people can exercise their skills, knowledge and capabilities to fullest extent possible then stepping back and letting it happen. The integrated term used for this process is called employees empowerment. Enabling means let go of control. A symbolic action can be a potent means of signaling that you have indeed let go. Enabling means that control must move all the way to the front/bottom line. A road block may encourage practicing old behavior. When employees becomes a part of the organization, they will develop ownership with their job, job place and organization as a whole and will put best efforts to contribute to the development of new ideas, new services, new products, new market and customers and will utilize their will to do their work and help others to do their work better and better. They will be fair, open and equitable in relationship within the organization. Ultimately they will do their work with quality and excellence. Employees will be more likely to buy into the new covenant if they are allowed to participate in any resolution of disputes.

Integral to the success of Turnaround Management is the management of the smooth change process that will effectively communicate the changes in people, processes, products and systems. If the management of an organization does not change, the Turnaround Management (TAM) will stop in its tracks and today's organization can't afford to let that happen. The only way we are going to deliver on the full promise of Turnaround Management (TAM) is to start turning our mind-set by absorbing inputs on Turnaround Management (TAM) and converting it into workable outputs for improving the organizations.

Why Turnaround Management?

In the challenging economic times coupled with globalization and knowledge workers and boundary less market, more and more organizations are restructuring in order to remain competitive in their market while ensuring a sound and financial base. There are some systems indicating the needs for Turnaround management are:

- ❖ New skills and capabilities are needed to meet current or expected operational requirements.
- ❖ Accountability for results are not clearly communicated and measurable resulting in subjective and biased performance appraisal.
- ❖ Parts of the organization are significantly over or understaffed.
- ❖ Organizational communication is inconsistent, fragmented, and inefficient.
- ❖ Technology and or innovations are creating changes in workflow, production and people processes.
- ❖ Personnel retention and turnover is a significant problem.
- ❖ Workforce productivity is stagnant or deteriorating.
- ❖ Employee's moral and motivation is at low level.
- ❖ Business is on set of decline, loss of market share and revenue.
- ❖ More stress on measurement of performance through financial indicators and ingoing other performance indicators such as impact of environment, welfare of employees and corporate social responsibility and employees work-life balance.
- ❖ Existing business performance is long-lasting below its limits and so on.

It is therefore necessary, just as individuals need to renew their physical and psychological energy, so organizations also need to renew themselves periodically. Turnaround management brings about change that also brings about stress and conflict. It is important for management to be able to effectively lead its management team through challenging and turbulent times. Being able to predict how workforce will respond to stress and conflict is the key to managing Turnaround management smoothly.

Change has truly become an inherent and integral part of organizational life. Today several emerging trends are impacting organizational life. These trends are creating tension for organizational leaders and employees as they go through waves of changes in their organizations. These tensions at the same time, presenting opportunities as well as threats and if these tensions are not manage well, they will result in dysfunctional dire organizational outcome at the end. Effective approaches in organizational renewal will involve not one strategic Turnaround management but many alternatives and will require leaders and employees to develop greater resilience in comforting these tensions

Turnaround Management Some Challenges

Many organizations don't start big. Instead, they start in shops at basements with small budgets and skeletal staff. However, when the organization matures and grows, it becomes a little harder to follow the conventional human relation policies, production processes, outdated technologies and marketing tactics. Further, when organizations grow in a big way you may find that Turnaround Management or change management has been the most instrumental factor in bringing about this. Turnaround Management is the strategic process of redesigning one or more aspects of the organization. The process may be implemented due to number of different factors such as positioning the organization to be more competitive for expanding markets, creations of strategic business units (SBUs), collaborations, changed workforces, cultures and so on. Thus Turnaround Management is often a necessity in such circumstances especially when the organization has grown to the point where the original structure and systems can no longer efficiently manage its output and general interests. Such examples include the additional departments, processes, systems or deleting some existing ones which are not adding value to the organization. Therefore, Turnaround Management is seen as a positive sign of organization growth and is often welcome by those who wish to see the organization gain a larger financial share in changing economy.

Turnaround management is to improve business performance by showing managers and employees how to revolutionize their key operations, human relations, production processes, customer service, cost cutting, product development, right sizing, improved people performance etc. which affect the profit margin. So Turnaround management is a necessity for changing or re-arranging managerial work, the way we think about, organize, inspire, deploy, enable, measure and reward the value adding operational work. The Turnaround Management solution is to integrate the effect of men, material, machine and money in order to bring about positive results to the organization. Turnaround Management has proved to be extra-ordinarily popular by taking roots in Indian industries, Turnaround Management broadly covers objective issues such as culture (change management), issues of process and performance, issues of people, etc. The ultimate aim is that everyone must change. The changes will go deeper than the techniques employed. It touches nearly all what management/managers do, as well as those of the employees. It touches not only their sense of task but also their sense of themselves. Not just what they know, but how they think. Not just their way of seeing the world, but their way of living in the world (J.Champy).

Turnaround Management Design

For organizations to develop them often must undergo significant changes in their overall strategies, practices and operational tactics. As organizations evolve through various life cycles, its leaders and employees must be able to successfully align with Turnaround Management, so that they can evolve as well. That is why Turnaround Management analysis has become an important part of today workforce management.

Integral to the success of Turnaround Management is managing the change process smoothly in a manner that will communicate the changes in your people, process, products, systems and policies. Turnaround Management does not apply only to distressed companies but, in fact, can also help in any situation where direction, strategy or a general change in the way of working needs to be implemented. Therefore, Turnaround Management is closely related to change management. Generally, Turnaround Management goes through following stages (Jim Mayer):

1. The Evaluation and Assessment Stage

When businesses are set to decline through loss of market shares and revenues, old and outdated management practices, employees' strained relations, etc. are the reasons that cause the destabilization of an organization's performance.

2. Turnaround Situation

An organization's existing performance is long-lasting but may be below its limits, and this may be due to the ignorance of other performance indicators such as its impact on the environment, welfare of employees, work life balance and corporate social responsibility. So it is not always acceptable to measure performances through financial success indicators.

3. Search for New Strategy/Strategies

Most of the focus on the structure and its impact on performance of the strategy that was implemented may not be scientific (short term solutions) in changing economic, social environment.

4. Implications of New Strategy/Strategies

Does an outcome of the new strategies turnout to be good then turnaround shall be successful. This is achieved when its appropriate benchmark reaches the level of commercial success, like it was a case before the onset of business decline. The results are commonly measured in the time frame between two and four years. (as short term and long term goals).

5. Selection of New Strategy to Decide

What way problematic areas are to be prioritise for finding out right solution to the problem. It may be structure, strategy, style, shared skills and shared values or operational production processes, problems or marketing problems or key strategic critical performance factors, key performance areas or non-value adding departments and their activities or overall business units which are turned into question mark or stray dog zone, where draining out of revenue is visible. Depending on the depth of the problem, strategic intent is to be formulated before going for action. This can be undertaken by business SWOT analysis.

After reviewing the situation in context with above five stages it is easier to decide what tools, techniques or incentives to be advocated for solving the problem. Tools or techniques may be downsizing/right sizing or smart sizing of people, processes or products or operating systems; replacement or renewal of the systems, producers or practices or creation of new department or renewed people management issues. Based on the above Turnaround management strategies/alternatives can be fixed up for overcoming the problems. Solutions to such problems can provide you with the means to easily align the goals of your employees to the overall mission of the organization and will help to develop an effective solution for Turnaround management by accessing workforce mind and their alignment to the following issues:-

- ❖ Overall vision, mission and strategy.
- ❖ Current and future business objectives.
- ❖ Functional/optional policies and systems.
- ❖ Key performance areas and key result areas.
- ❖ Performance management, measurement and development of people, processes and production processes.
- ❖ Formation of strategic business units (SBUs).
- ❖ Development of new systems, practices.

Since the business world is constantly changing, continuous organization's new learning is necessary to stay up-date. Organizations that cannot learn will become obsolete. Therefore, organization leaders should periodically examine the organization structure for their enterprise to assure that it continues to provide an environment for organizational learning. Organizations are human systems and their system structure includes beliefs, values, mental model of their organization leaders and his employees. Changing organizational behavior and improving performance requires change in behavior. Therefore, turnaround management have a fundamental goal to facilitation of clear, open communication that can enable organizational learning and clarify accountability for results.

II. ORGANIZATIONAL BEHAVIOR

Managers and employees in general need to develop their interactional or people skills to be effective in their jobs. Organizational behavior is a field of study that investigates the impact that individual, group and structure have on behavior within the organization. Organizational behavior focuses on inter-personal relations, group relations. There is growing awareness that the success of any organizations is directly dependent on the positive human relations. Organizational behavior is comparatively new discipline, describing, and understanding, predicting and controlling human behavior in a given organizational situations. It is a study of groups, group dynamics, group relations, individuals, team working, leadership and how organization functions and change is affected in organizational setting. Therefore, Organizational behavior can be considered as the study and application of knowledge about individuals and groups. It follows a system approach and interprets employee's organization relationship as a whole social system of the organization. Its purpose is to build better as well as positive relationships by achieving human objectives and social objectives. The organizational behavior approach helps investigate facts of areas like personality, perception, assumptions, attitudes, group dynamics, work satisfaction, leadership decision making, communication, company 'politics and power', company climate and culture.

Theorists like E. Mayo, Rithligberger, C.I. Banard, Bennis took centre stage in organizational behavior arena and postulated that the manager's role is not command and control employees but to facilitate employee participation and performance. They propagated that employees in the organization work to make their living, but their efforts go beyond just laboring. They also work to fulfill certain needs. eg contributing to organizational objectives, attaining feeling of accomplishment and using their creativity in the work environment. System theorist to organizational behavior also applied a five part system approach to organizational behavior e.g. the individual, the formal organization, the informal organization, the physical environment and the fusion process in which these four factors modify and shape one-another. This system approach is the basis of today organization theory, which is founded on the contribution of behavioral sciences like psychology (the study of human behavior), sociology (the study of social behavior), Anthropology (the study of the origin, cultural development and human behavior). Each science has made important contribution to study of organizational behavior. Psychologists are concerned with study of learning, participation, motivation, and attitude. Sociologists study the organization that composed society e.g. politics and power, legal business, government and finally Anthropologists are interested in the study of impact of culture on behavior. These studies have major impact on organizational behavior. These studies extensively contributed on the thinking of employer and employee in the organization. The process of unfreezing the current status of organizational behavior involves introducing new changes, policies or initiatives that began to actively move employers and employees away from the old way of doing things. Today, the global economy has taken on added importance in organizational behavior circle as global companies have special requires and dynamics to contend with such researchers now concentrating such things as communication between and among foreign business operation methods, cultural differences and their impact on individual's language, difficulties, motivation techniques, differences in leadership style and decision making practices from country to country. They are busy to study how such factors will affect organizational behavior and what can be done to alleviate associated problems.

The organization base ultimately rests on management philosophy, assumptions, values, vision, mission and business objectives. This in turn derives the organizational culture which is composed of formal and informal, social groups, structure and environment. These factors determine human relations, leadership behavior, communication, interpersonal relations, and group dynamics within the organization. Today employees perceive it as the quality of work life which in turn directs their degree of motivation, satisfaction personal and professional development. All these factors together build the model of organizational behavior operational in the organization. In short, these factors are very much influential in deciding organizational behavior. These are the factors help organizational people to understand and share expectation so that they can learn to supervise their own behavior, become responsible, self motivated, whether they are management leaders, managers or employees.

There is still much that is unknown about human behavior. But knowledge about motivation, attitude, behavior (present, past and future) and change will continue to be of great concern to organizational leaders for several reasons:

It can help to improve the effective utilization of human resources by their active participation and involvement. It will help preventing resistance to change, and often it will lead to more a productive organization. Knowing the basic concepts, techniques and practices of organizational behavior help management, managers and employees of organizational behavior immensely. The focus is also moving from a kind of maintenance of human element to more advanced and new fashioned organizational behavior. Therefore, organizational leaders not only need to be aware of these issues but also well versed in analysis, design and implementation of organizational behavior intervention. Understanding and implementing organizational behavior intervention can provide towards participative and collaborative management. The very survival of organization depends on its ability to move from present philosophy to philosophy of collaborative. Developing positive organizational behavior by positive inter-personal, inter group relations, involving employees, deciding on systems change in consultation with employees and thus enhancing participation for development of holistic relationship at work. Organizational behavior interventions like works committee, task force, think tank, quality circles; Kaizen team etc can give voluntary participation and involvement to employees. When they are allowed to find out solutions to their workplace. Problem with freehand, their self actualization need will be fulfilled and they will be proud of their workmanship. Such organizational behavior interventions focus a developmental view of individuals, teams and organization that seeks to betterment of both employees and organization. By working to improve organizational behavior an organization can enhance employee commitment. Employee job satisfaction improves based on the level of commitment to the organization and job responsibilities. Through communication, an employee can become more aware of the organizational strategy. This allows the employees to feel empowered to act on behalf of the company. As employees become more empowered, the behavior of the organization improves.

III. ORGANIZATION DEVELOPMENT (OD)

Organizations must be able to meet present and future challenges put up by global economy. And for this organizations must be adaptable and responsive ever ready. In such situation, organizations must seek change in doing their conventional things again and again. The fast pace of change itself which demands organizations to be extremely flexible in order to survive and prosper. Organizational development attempts to develop the whole organization so that it can respond to change more uniformly and capably. In short, organizational development's objective is to change all parts of organization in order to make it more humanly responsive, more effective and more capable for renewal. Organizational leader single handedly, in isolation can't do this. He has to involve and empower individuals and various teams in the organization. Because organizational development interventions have some basic assumptions about people at work:-

- Most people have drives toward personal growth and this is most likely to be actualized in an environment which is supportive, collaborative, participative and challenging.
- Most people wish to be accepted and to interact cooperatively within group and usually more than one group in the organization. One of the most psychologically relevant reference group for most people is the work group, including peers and superior.
- Most people are capable of greatly increasing their effectiveness in helping reference group to solve problems effectively working together.

- For a group to promise its effectiveness the formal group (superiors) can't perform all of the leadership functions in all circumstances at all times. Obviously, all group members assist each other with effective leadership and member's behavior.

Based on these assumptions on organizational development intervention organizational transformation is possible by:-

- Empowering employees to do their jobs to the best of their abilities which requires pushing authority, responsibility and information downward.

- Empowering employees to change the existing systems of doing the work replacing it with more positive and effective systems. P. Drucker rightly said that, "most problems are caused not by employees, but by systems, technologies and processes since these are designed by people. It only make sense that allowing people to fix problems in system, technologies and processes will have tremendous impact in increasing productivity and quality."

- Providing clear vision to people and helping everyone to understand the organizational strategy to motivate people as they are not working at cross purposes. Organizational change happens weather we know it or not. Organizational change can be choice however if we are proactive rather than reactive.

Any organizational change or organizational development needs to be owned at the top level in an appropriate way throughout the organization. Sometimes top down other time bottom up depending on the structure and existing culture, climate and commitment of organization leader. Organizational development response to change. Change in individual attitude and behavior is a primary target of organizational development. It is a behavioral approach emphasizes the better utilization of human resources by improving the level of motivation, morale, and commitment of all employees. Organizational development is a system wise application and transfer of behavior and knowledge for a planned development, improvement and reinforcement of strategies, structure and processes (structural, technological and behavioral) that lead to organizational effectiveness. Obviously it requires skills in working with individuals, groups and whole organization. Organizational development is primarily driven by action research. The practice of organizational development is grounded in a distinctive set of core values and principles that guide organization's behavior and actions.

These values are:-

- **Respect And Inclusion** – Give equal values, perspective and opinions of everyone.
- **Collaboration** – Participate, involve to build win-win situation in the organization.
- **Authencity** – To help people behave congregant with their espoused values.
- **Self awareness** – Committed to developing self awareness and interpersonal skills within the organization.
- **Empowerment** – To focus on helping everyone in organization, increase individual level of autonomy and sense of personal power and courage in order to enhance productivity and elevate employee morale.
- **Democratic and social justice** – The belief that people will support those things for which they have had in shaping that human spirit is elevated by perusing democratic principles.

In summary, the price of changing people and organization activities with changed attitudes and behaviours for positive growth is organizational development. It is a process of developing organization to be more effective and flexible in accomplishing its desired goals. It is planned interventions aimed at improving individual and organizational health. It is also long-term effort lead and supported by top management to improve an organizational visioning, empowerment, learning, problem solving through on-going collaborative management of organizational culture. By inviting employee's participation and involvement, organizational change can be carried out smoothly by undertaking initiatives like team building, carrier development, coaching, training, quality improvement, innovation, leadership development and change management. Organizational development is an attempt to influence the employees of an organization to expand their candidness with each other about their views of the organization and their experience in it to take greater responsibility for their own actions as organization members. The assumptions behind organizational development is that when people pursue both of these objectives simultaneously, they are likely to discover and experience new ways of working together that would effectively result in the achievement of their shared (organizational) goals. When this does not happen, such activities help them to understand why it is necessary to make meaningful choices about what to do in light of this understanding.

– (Neilson)

Organizational leaders need to develop their skills in structural, behavioral, directive and participative change strategies as well as to maintain their skills in inter-personal participative management so that the movement towards self renewing organization can begin with some scope of success.

IV. INDIVIDUAL AND ORGANIAZTIONAL LEARNING (I&OL)

If you want to build a continuously improving organization, you need to build a continually learning organization, An erudite guru has rightly pin-pointed that, "An organization needs people that are improving with education so that it promotes learning as a way of business life for employees and organization." Yet, giving people plenty of education, information, inspiration and awareness will prove futile if they don't have skills to improve the quality of the product or service. This will cause them to become frustrated and de-motivated. Awareness and empowerment are useless without enablement and involvement. The success of organizational efforts on learning and employee development will have direct proportion to your investment. Employee learning and development is one of the vital parts of the organization. It is amazing to see that the transition that takes place once you give people/employees the tools, confidence, freedom and trust to unleash their potential through their participation, involvement, knowledge, power so pays to invest in employees learning and development. Employees learning will upgrade their native-skills, new skills, capability, get engaged with enthusiasm to achieve higher retention, improve employee morale and motivation, work flexibility thus will enhance organization's competitive edge. It is known that unless learning is equal to or greater than change an organization will become extinct. Therefore, active learning by both individual and organization are pre-requisites for survival, success in any business. It is not world-class talent, it is world-class talent performance as we are experiencing with highly empowered companies like Infosys, Wipro, Mahindra and Mahindra, Unilever, Godrej tec.

Employee development is an investment in building positive behaviours, attitudes, knowledge and skills that will result in successful performances and other desired goals of the organization. Employees and managers are partners in the development processes. Employees are responsible for their own development. Management/managers provide information, education and opportunities for employees to develop in a supportive and participative environment. Cumulative learning of individuals, teams and organizations influences talent through the applications of knowledge for the improvement of organizational performance. Key components of individual learning for organizational development are founded on positive, participative and organizational and collective behaviours. Employee learning mainly encompasses developmental planning, performance assessments, skill developments, carrier planning and record management.

These are key strategic principles of employee complexity and organization learning. Organizations need continuous learning for at least four reasons:-

1. Organizations are dealing with the increasing complexity of managing in multi-cultural and multi-national environments and uncertain economic climate.

2. Ambiguity is often high because of complex system. In such situation, organizational existence is not predictable and thus not controllable.

3. Way of working become more fluid with the advent of electronic communication technologies, allowing for instance, geographical dispersed teams and employee market in different part of world.

4. Organizations have moved heavily from a manufacturing age to service age and are now moving to knowledge age and creating knowledge requires continuous learning. Therefore, the need to learn continuously and the need to encourage the learning of employees who make the organization. If they don't they will not be able to keep pace with their competitors. Goals and obstacles in environment establish the need for continuous learning. The need may arise from any trigger or disturbance in the environment which could include such things as new competitor, a change in task because of new technology or a new idea that needs to be brought into fruition such as developing a new product or creating a new market.

Learning at the individual, group and organizational level can be adaptable, generative and or transformative. Adaptive learning is reacting to change in the environment. Generative learning is for generating new knowledge and applying frame breaking ideas and bringing about radically new conditions, environmental demands for learning and the capability or readiness of the individual group and organization to alter components of themselves, learning, is necessary. People throughout the organization must become involved in learning also play greater role in both formulation and implementation of organization strategies and tactics. Put another way, to learn and adapt, organization needs eyes, ears and brains – all people. One person or small group of individuals can no longer think and learn for the entire entity. Therefore, it requires collective/organizational learning is pivotal to success in rapidly changing environments. Organizational leaders must play a key role in setting the tone. Facilitating organizational learning represents the process by which the organizations learn by experience about how to move effectively manage its core value creating activities and use its physical and financial resources. Although learning process certainly involve an organizational human resources directly, rather cumulative learning influences human element through the application of knowledge and the involvement and enhancement of the organizational structure, systems and the processes.

Organizational learning refers to the capacity of an organization to change and improve continuously. Organizational learning helps organization to move beyond the current situation by solving problems and ultimately transforming the organization. It results in the development of a learning organization where empowered employees take responsibility for strategic direction. Organizational learning at the core of its nation is the belief that organizational learning provides a number of advantages. Some of those advantages include improved individual and team performance, enhanced product/service quality, new product development, better quality work life and ultimately competitive advantage. There is wide spread acceptance that learning could occur at the individual, team and organizational level. Understanding of learning orientations at these three levels has the capacity to advance knowledge and practice of organizational learning. It is proved that individual learning and group learning is significantly related to organizational learning. Through organizational learning, an organization gain knowledge and develops skills to empower its employees to work as cohesive team. Implementing organizational learning is to implement team learning where employees are willing and able to work together to build new mind-set and transfer knowledge throughout the organization or requires creating, acquiring, transferring and retaining knowledge and modifying current collective behavior to increase organizational efficiency. An organization's skill is found in its accepted behavior patterns and its collective knowledge logged in its shared assumptions. The organizational attitude exists in the core value. If these can be developed within an individual employee, there is no reason why this can't happen for an organization. It might be more difficult and take longer time, but the existence of organizational learning can't be decried.

Learning strategies for creating a continues learning environment thus requires two phase learning; Individual and organizational learning. Individual learning is the ability of individual employee to pursue self-development. It requires employees take personal responsibility for their own learning and development through process of assessment, reflection and action. Individual learning helps the employees continually update and remain marketable in the workplace. Organizational learning occurs when the entire organization addresses and solves problems, builds repositories of lessons learned and creates core competencies that present the collective learning of employee's past and present. Organizational learning not only contributes to resolving organizational issues but promotes individual development of knowledge, skills and competencies.

Human resources is the engine behind the creation of all values:-products and services are conceived, designed, manufactured and sold by people through those individuals skills, knowledge, competencies, and abilities. So we must aware to draw a connection between developing talent and fulfillment of organization strategies. Their potential (learning output) to organization and its people sounds favorable for achieving organizational performance. It is to be noted that organization learns only through the learning of employees. Trust them, develop, participate and involve and empower them to bring new ideas for overall organizational improvement.

In summary in individual and organizational learning, it is a group of people working together to collectively enhance their capacities to create results that they truly care about. (peter Senge). The strength of organizational and individual learning is that the more they know the faster they learn. As business environment speeds up organizational learning must match its acceleration. As business relationships become more multifaceted and complex the nature of what the organization needs to learn becomes more difficult. Strategic organizational learning becomes the process by which an organization makes sense of its environment by broadening and sustaining the range of objectives it can pursue and the range of resources and actions available to faster organizational objectives. (Sancher and Heene – 1997). Building on our belief of organizational learning, the learning organization would appear to be an organization that provides an environment conducive to knowledge creation, growth and sharing through the nurturing of living networks. It facilitates the flow of understanding through the use of teams and supports, encourages and values individual learning. It builds and sustains systems and processes that support knowledge centricity and develops systems and process to sustain organizational memory. Organizational learning always ensures personal and professional learning of the individuals within the organization but also ensures individual's learning on how to collaborate and create synergisms of knowledge and practice, at the systems or teams level. Organizational learning is accelerated when an organization through knowledge manage, create a common knowledge redepository and identifies and codifies competencies and routines including acquiring, storing, interpreting and manipulating information from within and external to the organization. Simultaneously, knowledge sharing processes – leveraging both by individual and organizational learning improve the quality and speed of communication and the understanding of problems and changes surrounding the organization, increasing the quality of decisions and effectiveness of their implementation.

V. KNOWLEDGE MANAGEMENT (KM)

In machine age human element in organization was ancillary. Things were central-products, capital budget, plant and equipment etc. But today the knowledge driven economy returns to the effective management of human element is likely to exceed those available from more efficient management of financial and physical assets. In order to realize returns however, organizations must go beyond productivity and profitability by developing and implementing new approaches and management techniques to tap the knowledge, intellect and creativity of human resources. In today's economy it is one of the major resources improves the utilization of financial and physical aspects boosting overall organization's performance. "Knowledge Management" and know-how embodied in organization's human resources presents a whole new set of challenges for management and managers.

"(Hamel Prahalad) First of all on economic front, knowledge is a unique kind of resource, in that it is not consumed is use but grows more valuable and more productive as it is shared and re used. Peter Drucker has rightly pointed out that" future economic growth can no longer be based on expanding the workforce or increasing consumer demands, rather, it can only from a very sharp and continuing increase in productivity of one resource: knowledge work and knowledge worker. Human capital includes the know-how, capabilities, abilities, skills, competencies and expertise of organization's employees.

Knowledge Management (KM) develops systems and processes to acquire and share intellectual assets. It increases the generation of useful, actionable and meaningful information and seeks to increase both individual and team learning. In addition, it can maximize the value of an organization's intellectual base across diverse functions. Knowledge Management maintains that successful businesses are a collection of not of products but of distinctive knowledge base. The intellectual capital is the key that will give the organization a competitive advantage with its targeted customers. Knowledge Management of organization seeks to accumulate intellectual capital that will create unique core competencies and lead to superior results. Today, everywhere you look our systems are under pressure, whether it is social, economic, political or organizational systems. The world we grew up is changing as never before. Behind this change is the growth of knowledge as a vital economic resource. Organizations that pursue broad and systematic knowledge management find that several practices that in total contribute to the overall organization success. Organizations are now vigilant in their focus on using following practices as chief enablers for success.

- ❖ Foster knowledge (supportive culture) characteristics of general nature include safe working, ethical and mutually respectable behavior, collaboration and a common focus on delivering quality work.
- ❖ Shared understanding-developing a broadly shared understanding of the organization's vision mission and the role of employees in support of the enterprise and of the individuals own interest.

❖ Focus on knowledge management practice to align with organization direction. Knowledge management identifies the intended business direction of the organization to ascertain that the associated knowledge related factors receive appropriate attention and are well maintained.

❖ Practice accelerated learning-pursue a broad range of knowledge transfer activities to ascertain that valuable knowledge is captured, organized and structured, developed widely used and leveraged.

To make these practices effective, organizations to pursue following success factors for building organizations knowledge management.

- **Knowledge And Resources** – Professional knowledge, information and other necessary resources must be made available for employees to deliver quality work, products and services that satisfy the requirements of the situation and general service paradigm. Employee must also possess requisite skills, attitude and behavior and other personality traits. They must be supported in their abilities to think critically and creatively in being provided with relevant meta-knowledge.

- **Extend Participation** – Employees must be provided safe environment in which to do their work. That means they must be given permission to innovate, improvise and sketch organizational policies and practices beyond pre-determined scope to serve the organization and the stake holders best interest. Their participation and involvement will empower them to do the right things beneficial to the organization.

- **Motivate them** – Employees must be motivated to act intelligently to do the right things by providing with the understanding and emotional acceptance of how their actions will be of value to the organization and employees in general. This requires active two-way communication.

- **Continuous Training** – Employees training and development is resourceful for their career planning and progression. This also helps to develop core competencies of employees and stability of manpower retention is also of advantage to organization.

These factors if implemented systematically will help for evaluation of organizational knowledge:

- Knowledge development through learning, training, coaching, mentoring, innovations, creativity and improvement.
- Knowledge refinement – It is organized, transformed or included in written documents, manuals, reports and so on to make it available to use.
- Knowledge leveraging – It is applied or otherwise leveraged in using, applying knowledge and it becomes the basis for further learning and innovation an explained by mechanisms like quality, quality circle, kaizen, self-managed teams etc. comprehensive evolution of knowledge management processes will then follow the following sub-processes:
  o Deploy knowledge to people, practices, technology, products and services.
  o Apply, use and leverage knowledge to act effectively for viability and success.
  o Create knowledge, learn, innovate and research by using prior and imported knowledge.
  o Capture and store knowledge to build, revise and leverage it in other way.
  o Organize and transform knowledge to make it broadly available and embed it.
  o Tap and use (tacit knowledge) personal knowledge, experience, skills of employees as knowledge bank. They may have strong meta-knowledge that provides capabilities to make sense of novel situations and create effective approaches for organizational well beings.

A useful way to conceptualize our knowledge management strategy is through people, processes and technology. While there is a greater consensus emerging in favor of the first-people in the organization, who are the ones that create, share and use knowledge. Without taking into account of people's play in generating and sharing knowledge, no organization can develop into comprehensive knowledge management bank. It is therefore, necessary to participate, involve and empower employees in organization's affairs.

Knowledge management is a discipline of enabling individual employees, teams and entire organization to collectively and systematically create, share and apply knowledge to better achieve their objectives. Unwritten, unspoken and hidden vast store house of knowledge held by practically every normal human beings based on his emotions, experiences, insight, induction, observations and internalized information. Tacit knowledge is integral to the entirety of person's consciousness and is acquired largely through association with other people and requires joint or shared activities to be imparted from one to another. Like submerged part of an ice-berg it constitutes the bulk of what one knows and forms knowledge possible. Managing tacit knowledge is a significant challenge in the business world and it requires more awareness of barriers. For example, during the new idea generation, divergent thinking phase people create a wealth of possible solution to a problem. Chaos succeeds in creating newness because it takes place in a system that is non-liner. In a well managed development process, where group or diverse individuals address a common challenge, varying perspectives, foster creative abrasion, intellectual conflict between diverse viewpoints producing energy that is channelized into new ideas. Mechanism by which such collective tacit knowledge is created and tapped include brain storming, nominal group techniques, critical mass technique becomes the starting point in the organizational learning.

There is a clear understanding across the industries that the mining of tacit knowledge (personal knowledge) is the base for redefining explicit knowledge of the organization. Fifty percent of the organization's (corporate) knowledge is housed exclusively in the brains of its employees. The winner in the knowledge base-economy will be those organizations that understand returns on time-the ability to leverage what they know to respond more quickly than their competitors. Thus two-way exchange of opportunities, information benefits both individual and organization. Individual knowledge, skills and capabilities can be enhanced by encouraging and facilitating individual learning and providing opportunities for training, skill development. Employee's participation and involvement will empower them to solve organizational problems with free mind and with the sense of ownership of the organization.

Getting together a set of employees with diverse skills bring together to generate new ideas, stay focused on the topic and think outside the box. Management, managers and teams can use tacit knowledge to aid convergent thinking by creating, guiding vision, mission concepts for teams involved in innovation and creativity. Quality circles, joint councils, quality improvement teams, safety committee etc. such committees/teams go together with tacit knowledge collection so that it can leverage an explicit knowledge (organization knowledge) that becomes more accessible across the organization.

For organization's improvement there are four abilities that are critical for organization development.; Cognitive skills of people, self-knowledge, emotional resilience and personal drive. To develop these meta-abilities understanding organizational roles, internal strengths and formal and informal discussion, participation and rational discourse are necessary factors. This is because all these factors are more focused upon developing employee communication, conflict resolution, team building, cooperativeness, persuading others (leadership) and managing organizational politics-which are relevant to achieve the objectives of the organization. Considering the above it confirms that employee development.

VI TOTAL QUALITY MANAGEMENT (TQM)

    i.   **WHAT IS TOTAL QUALITY MANAGEMENT**
    ii.   **EVOLUTION OF TOTAL QUALITY MANAGEMENT**
    iii.   **CONTRIBUTORS TO TOTAL QUALITY MANAGEMENT**

   iv.   **CATEGORIES OF TOTAL QUALITY MANAGEMENT**
   v.   **APPROACHES TO TOTAL QUALITY MANAGEMENT**
   vi.   **BUILDING BLOCKS OF TOTAL QUALITY MANAGEMENT**

Empowering employees is the basic principle of total quality management. Empowerment is an environment in which people have the ability, confidence and the commitment and ownership to improve the processes and initiate the necessary steps to satisfy customer requirements within well-defined boundaries in order to achieve organizational values and goals (Bester field). The approach places the responsibility for an organization's processes in the hands of those (employees) who know these processes best and help them to participate directly in organization's mission and purpose. Under total quality management continuous improvement by those in a process and this introduces elements of bottom-up issues identification and problem solving. As a result, total quality management empower employees by delegating functions that were previously the preserve of senior management and as a result, institutionalize participation on permanent basis. (Hill 1991). Empowered and involved employees know how to do better and incorporate their skills in day-to-day work-tasks and thus they can exercise better judgment and a sense of responsibility. Finally, a supportive organizational culture is the common denominator of all soft aspects of total quality management. As still points out that it nurtures high trust social relationships and it develops a shared sense of membership as well as belief that continuous improvement is for the good of everyone within an organization.

It is widely accepted that the increase of employee participation is the overall strategy brings an increased flow of information and knowledge and contributes in the distribution of intelligence to the bottom of the organization for resolving problems (Powell, 1995). Oakland pointed out that "Total quality management is essentially a way of organizing, involving the whole organization, every department, every activity, every single person at every level." From the soft concepts of total quality management like total employee involvement, continuous training employee empowerment, team work, continuous improvement, top management commitment, democratic management style and culture change, all these elements are getting resolved around employees in the organization.

What Is Total Quality Management?

Total Quality Management is an integrative philosophy of management for continuously improving quality of products, processes and people. Total Quality Management works on the premise that the quality of products and processes is the responsibility of every employee who is involved with the creation of products or services, offered by an organization. In other words, Total Quality Management capitalizes on the involvement of employees, suppliers and customers (Wikipedia). In Total Quality Management, all members of an organization participate in improving processes, products, services and the culture in unison they work. Total Quality Management is the culture of an organization committed to customer's satisfaction – internal and external through continues improvement. In essence, Total Quality Management is the mutual cooperation of every employee in an organization and associated with business to produce products and services when meet and hopefully, exceed the needs and expectations of customers. Total Quality Management is both a philosophy and a set of management guiding principles for managing an organization

– **(Dale)**

Total Quality is an approach to improve the effectiveness and flexibility of an organization as a whole. This is possible only when each function and each person develops an attitude for quality to prevent and eliminate errors, waste, rework etc. Team work, participation, involvement and communication are key factors can be achieved by creating the cultural change in an organization. To improve total quality a culture has to be promoted where employees feel free to contribute their ideas for organizational problem solving. One of the important elements in building quality oriented culture is the attitude of people. And it is the job of management to get message across through employees participation, involvement and empowerment that quality is an important corporate strategic consideration.

Evolution of Total Quality Management

Total Quality Management is an evolutionary concept. It has nature, philosophy and titles have changed with time. Its evolution could be traced back from the stages of inspection, control, assurance. Each of these stages reflects a change in the market conditions, customer requirements and employees involvement. Inspection phase directed to carry out inspection and measurement to segregate the good output from the unequality which is not conforming to laid down parameters. During this phase quality was regarded as inspection only. This reflected a business culture prevalent at that time which was based on output optimization and profit at any cost.

Quality Control Phase – Quality control phase focused on product defects detection through post-production inspection. It was concerned with the adherence to standards and sorting out rejects. Quality continued to be regarded as an end of line function where attention was given more to end product than the processes themselves. Variation was studied through a decision making process based on acceptable or un acceptable standards.

Quality Assurance Phase – It recognizes that inspection is not the answer and that the entire manufacturing process must be committed to meeting the quality needs of the customer. Quality assurance contains all those planned and systematic actions required to provide adequate confidence that a product or service will satisfy given requirements for quality. Quality Assurance focuses on procedure compliance and product conformity to specifications through production and operations management, often using statistical process control (SPC) as a tracking tool. The quality assurance also means that there is a set of documentation (a system) which demonstrates the existing standards of quality and reliability. The system for the implementation, controlling and auditing in quality assurance is often open to third party approval either by customers or government or any other agencies.

Total Quality Management (TQM) Phase – When quality assurance philosophy is expanded beyond manufacturing operations into other areas of organizational life, it is termed as total quality control (TQC). Total quality control has been described as "a management framework to ensure continuing excellence, concerns with direct cost reduction and a pre-occupation with efficiency are ousted in favor of the pursuit of quality through the elimination of waste and non-value added procedures." Total quality control is supported to be a company-wide movement but, actually, is largely limited to the manufacturing function. Total quality management (TQM) is a fundamental shift from what has gone before. Total quality management is that aspect of the overall management function that determines and implements the quality policy and as such is the responsibility of the top management. Total quality management is not therefore, a question of achieving standards but one of the survival and being strong all the time. Total quality management therefore, is an organizational concern and is driven by the culture of the organization. In total quality management, a customer orientation achieved through continuous quality improvement becomes a valid taken for granted, atmosphere shared by everyone, unquestioned and habitually enacted.

Total quality management has emerged as one of the most integrative mechanisms of organization development and improvement. It represents a complete way of managing an organization with a focus on quality and customer. The modern commercial world demands that organizations must continuously strive to improve the efficiency of their operations. Quality, therefore, has become a corporate strategy of doing business. It is no longer an opinion, it is a positive requirement. Today, many organizations recognize that they have to change the way they manage their businesses because their traditional customer bases are being eroded. They realize that they have to become competitive and therefore have to follow the leaders in businesses who seek total quality in every sense.

It therefore becomes obvious that employees are a fundamental component within any successfully developing organization. Take away people and the organization is nothing. Take away people's motivation, commitment and ability to work together in well organized teams and again the organization is nothing. Conversely, inspire people to work well, creatively and productively and the organization can progress. Logically, therefore, (PIE Interventions in Action | 181) the development and proper utilization of people are vital to the success of all quality management initiatives. People, culture, communications, commitments, systems, processes and interfaces are needed to change the culture of organization to ensure Total Quality Management. The failure to address the culture of an organization is frequently the reason for many management initiatives some of which have limited successes or are total failures. Understanding the culture of an organization and using that knowledge to successfully map the steps needed to accomplish a successful change is an important part of the quality journey. The culture of an organization is formed through its beliefs, behaviours, norms, dominant values, rules and climates. A cultural change, e.g. from an acceptance of errors or defects to one of error-less efficiency needs two elements:

- Commitment of organization leaders.
- Involvement of all of the organization.

There is wide-spread recognition that major change initiatives will not be successful without a culture of good team work and cooperation at all levels of an organization.

Contributors – The Masters of Quality

The concepts, philosophies, or theories developed by these quality gurus are by no means all the possible approaches to total quality management. These are the most important paradigm-shifting milestones on the quality adventure until now. There are dozens of different approaches organizations can implement under total quality management. Because each organizations operates with different types of people, in different climate, in different market and in different type of environments, and has different levels of sophistication and maturity. As a result, no one of these gurus have universal answer for everybody. Their contribution are just become guidelines that need to be shaped according to each organization. Let us see in brief their advocated philosophies.

W. Edwards Deming – An American, who advocated the plan-Do-Check-Act (PDCA) cycle. Quality through constancy through purpose, no inspection, continues improvement, barrier less communication, pride in workmanship, constant training is his contribution to quality.

Joseph M. Juran – An American, who initiated quality control, and advocated that quality must be integral part of management, quality is not accident, quality must be planned. There is no short-cut to quality, use problems as sources of improvement is his teaching in quality.

Philip B. Crasby – An American quality guru who propagated four absolutes of quality: Conformance to requirements; quality is achieved through prevention not appraisal; quality standard is zero defects, not acceptable level and quality is measured by the price of non-conformance. He advocated zero defects concept.

Genichi Taguchi – A Japanese who studied and implemented robust design concept. He say study all factors that can hamper uniformity between products and their long-term stable performance and build- in-safe guards at the product design itself. In other words, robust design.

Kaoru Ishikawa – Japanese quality thinker who advocated quality is a company-wide issue and must be all pervasive influence in the way every aspect of business is conducted. Seven simplified tools of quality control to be used by all people in an organization. Quality circle is one of the important concepts initiated by him to propagate quality management.

Shigeo singo – He pioneered the Just-In-Time concept which is applicable to moving goods, components and documents to correct and useful places only at a time when the movement needs to take place. The Zero-defects concept eliminates the source of error in each task so that it is impossible to perform the task wrongly. He advises the single minute exchange of die sub-concept which dismisses the machine set-up time through the use of proper design of equipment.

Based on these contributions of quality gurus, we can integrate their contributions under six broad categories to analyse total quality management. These broad categories help us understand the holistic theory covering every dimension of total quality management. The categories are:

Dibuffering – Check the buffers in your processes and remove them to run a tighter shop floor. SPC slashes tolerance buffers. Total quality control, by turning departments and functions into steps in a cross-functional processes, cut function or department buffers and quality circles eliminate authority buffers. Secondly, people needed training because it was not their product anymore; they were just working for someone else. An important thing about quality, therefore, is shaping attitude so that they will always be willing to do the best work or service possible. The ultimate aim of a dibuffering approach to remove buffer that stands between the employee and his work and in his mind.

Scientific Styling – These approaches use the scientific methods to satisfy the customer rather than generate knowledge. Taguchi's theories are a prime examples of this school. So is the quality approach termed total preventive maintenance which cuts equipment. Variation by systamatisizing every maintenance function.

Work force Deployment – Entire workforce shares in company policy-making function on quality. Their suggestions, ideas, innovations have to be treated with respect. Their suggestions are a breath-taking proof as regards the calibre of the ideas of the work forces, which can solve potential problems of the company. Total quality management is basically the respect for human beings; it is the respect for individuals. Most of the time we tell people to do what we want them to, instead of asking them to use their brains to perform a given function.

Process Engineering – Process architecting takes a fresh look at every process in the organization. It drops unnecessary processes and introduces them where there are none. Wherever necessary, a total redesign is implemented to free processes from sequential dependency on one another. When a total company uses a process engineering approach, it counts on the process to improve the quality of the products as well as the business. The principle of total quality can be applied to the process of implementing total quality. So a process engineering approach in a total quality organization is a self-nourishing and self-touting.

Organizational Transparency – Once company starts on quality path, it also needs to recognize its internal dynamics to be sensitive to the same sort of feelings and aspirations that its employees have. It needs to extend personal touch to everyone to facilitate the unhindered emotional transmission that adds value to every transaction.

Cognitive Competitiveness – New technologies, the rapid pace of change, global competition and use of quality practices themselves are making institutionalized continuous learning as one of the basic success factors. When organizations become self-perpetuating organisms of integrating individual, social, organizational memories, perceptions and skills into quality. When perception capability becomes the competitive edge, no process capability.

In nutshell, the total quality management philosophy entails empowered employees to solve problems independently. To bind the workforce, to give them a free hand, they must have the power to execute the solutions that they develop. Frontline staff must be able to redress complaints without running for approval to the boss. To build a quality empire – empower.

Approaches to Total Quality Management

Based on the theories, philosophies of quality gurus, there are about twenty four total quality management approaches categorized in six broad (as above) categories. Depending on the company culture, capabilities any approaches suitable to such company can be made applicable. The total quality management approaches are:

1. **Just-In-Time** – Cutting inventory buffers: raw materials, work-in-progress, finished goods, time, knowledge (dibuffering category).

2. **Statistical Process Control (SPC)** – Cutting tolerance through tighter monitoring of operations plan-do-check act cycle (dibuffering).

3. **Quality Circles** – Cutting authority buffers by empowering work force to develop solution (Dibuffering).

4. **Total quality Control** – Cutting departments/functions buffers by turning departments/functions into steps in a cross-functional process (debuffering).

5. **Total Preventive Maintenance** – Scientific prevention through systematized care of equipments (scientific styling).

6. **Statistical And Management Tools** – Histrogram, check sheets, cause and effect diagrams, affinity diagrams etc. (scientific styling).

7. **Robust Design** – Scientific design by maximizing signal to noise rate for long term stable performance (scientific styling).

8. **High Technology Circles** – Application of high technology tools like expert systems, multivariate statics, contradiction analysis (scientific styling).

9. **Automation Development** – Automating already laid down quality processes to buy time for work force to improve on these processes (work force deployment).

10. **Quality Function Deployment** – Mapping customer wants directly to all activities in the organization (work force deployment).

11. **New Technology Development** – Using new technology in organization before the old one becomes obsolete (work force deployment).

12. **Policy Deployment** – Involving the entire work force in the policy making function of a company (work force deployment).

13. **Process Architecting** – Refounding the work force from scratch for heightened quality (process engineering).

14. **Process Deployment Automation** – Automating the process, engineering process across the organization (process engineering).

15. **Process Improvement** – Analyzing the process of a business architecture to improve them (process engineering).

16. **Process Execution Automation** – Automating the routine processes across the entire organization (process engineering).

17. **Customer-Aided-Design** – Transferring the product design function to customers instead of relying on gut-feel (Organizational Transparency).

18. **Kansee Engineering** – Extending organizational systems till they can respond to emotional data from customers (Organizational Transparency).

19. **Customer Minded Corporation** – Getting customer to manage the company's systems and processes (Organizational Transparency).

20. **Middle-Up-Down Management** – Putting company systems in the hands of generation other than those usually in control (Organizational Transparency).

21. **Cognitive Quality of Work Life** – Defining company's ability to think, learn and invent in terms of customer requirement (cognitive competitiveness).

22. **Social Democratic Quality** – Management style based on the way university research work groups tend to operate (cognitive competitiveness).

23. **Mega-Cognitive organization** – Measuring and improving the cognitive process at all levels of the organization (cognitive competitiveness).

24. **Democratic Scientific Management** – The meta-quality corporation where every employee can improve cognitive processes (cognitive competitiveness).

These different total quality management approaches can be used by different organizations on a step-by-step basis in order to reach the total quality management target.

Building Blocks of Total Quality Management

Total quality management is founded upon some assumptions based on reality experiences at the work place. We call it the building blocks of total quality management. The CEO of the company must commit his personal time, company resources and management personnel to ensure quality standards. The objective is to establish quality visions and translate them into mission statements and objectives for individual employees. Don't just participate be involved. Based on CEO commitments, total quality management can be implemented in any organization, be it manufacturing or service. He must go through these total quality management building blocks before launching his total quality management journey as per his organizations capabilities. The total quality management building blocks are:

1. Turn employees from skill holders to disseminators; create learning enabling managers who develop, not filter people.
2. Emphasize process more than product.
3. Get people to perform mundane activities with full quality focus.
4. Measure key parameters of all activities.
5. Use technology efficiently.
6. Build in continuous learning and improvement process.
7. Get the workforce to manage it self.
8. Use customer and competitor to drive all decisions.
9. Use sincerity and trust as basis for all dealings, saying is doing.
10. Deploy the whole work force.
11. Benchmark against best – of the breed companies and copy best practices.
12. Use facilitation, mediate structure to bring the change.
13. Compensate for weakness inherent in culture.
14. Maintain all time focus on objectives: to satisfy customers better than competitors do.
15. Use scientific methods. Not opinion or gut-feel.
16. Use cross functional people and cross functional teams.

Thus, taking quality out of shop floor to encompass every conceivable activity in an organization with the customer-internal and external at the centre of all thoughts, processes, decisions. All it means really is a collection of all the things that we must do to have quality leadership. Born on shop floor, quality management has been transferred into a global framework for global business excellence that you ignore only at your peril.

VII. BUSINESS PROCESS RE-ENGINEERING (BPR)

The two cornerstones of any organization are the people and the processes. If individuals are motivated and working hard yet business processes are cumbersome and non-essential activities remain, organizational performance will be poor. Business process re-engineering is the key for transforming how people work. What appear to be minor changes in processes can have drastic effects on cash flow, service delivery and customer satisfaction. Business process re-engineering focuses on process and not on task, jobs. It endeavors to redesign the strategic and value added processes that transcend organizational boundaries.

Business process re-engineering is the concentration on the improvement of key business processes to ensure that output are delivered with speed, service and quality. Re-engineering is all about reinventing the entire organization-including people, structures rather than just processes. Organizations looking for radical improvement need business process re-engineering. Forget what your competitor is doing. Take, instead a clean sheet of paper and design your process the way you would have done it had you started from scratch. Redesigning, reengineering management processes and starting fresh enables on organization to identify the key business processes and ordinary processes. KBP's offer maximum value propositions to the customers. Ordinary business processes (OBP) offer little or no value propositions to customers. At the heart of business process re-engineering lies motion of discontinuous thinking. Organizations will have to identify and abandon old and obsolete rules and assumptions that underlie the current business practices. Hammer and J. Champy defined "business process re-engineering is the fundamental rethinking and radical redesign of business process to achieve dramatic improvement in critical contemporary measures of performance such as cost, quality, service and speed."

Any organization, irrespective of size, type or desired objective, operate fundamentally by transforming an amount of inputs (raw material or raw data) into required out-puts (product or services). This transformation involves one or more processes. Business processes are simply a set of activities that transform a set of inputs into a set of out puts. Improving business process is paramount importance to business to stay competitive in today's market place. The improvements in process quality that can be gained from business process re-engineering lies in three dimensions: Process efficiency (for example-cost, cycle time, yield), Product quality (measured-customer satisfaction, quality of product) and Product development business process re-engineering definitely can help the organization to get ahead of competitions in a big way only when its demands are well understood and carried out with the full participation and cooperation of employees. The willingness of the people to take up the challenges that are crucial for a successful business process re-engineering implementation is vital, rather than focusing on the factors that have traditionally received more attention, like resources. In summary, business process re-engineering is all about changing anything which proves to be a block to improving today's business performance, even if it means going back to the drawing board. (Obeng and Crainer-1994). Andrew and Stalick highlight the importance of the organizational integration aspects of business process re-engineering defining it as "radically changing how people work-changing business policies and controls, systems, structures, technology, organizational relationships and business practices. Because it encapsulates the key components of an organization and because it has shared values/culture at its centre," McKensey's Seven's'model may also be used to assess the impact of business process re-engineering on the organization.

1. **Systems** – Systems are codified knowledge, organized in a logical sequence. They are the processes, methods, procedures, rules, techniques, technology, manuals etc that ensure that work is undertaken efficiently. Systems are the instructions that guide

employees and management in their daily tasks. All business process re-engineering definitions either explicitly or implicitly refer to these attributes of systems.

2. **Structure** – How an organization breaks down its processes into distinct sub-processes and how these processes are coordinated depends on structure. And through business process re-engineering new or redesigned organization structure must accommodate a balance between financial expertise and process involvement. With the new process orientation in a redesigned organization structure it will incorporate attributes of the adhocracy. Employees may not be need to supervised. They are adults who are willing to take responsibility for their work, products and services.

3. **Staff** – The role of managers transformed. They will have new roles of teacher, guide, coach. Employees at other levels will be responsive to their roles. They will have a specialist role fundamentally.

4. **Skills** – The competencies the organization needs in its people in order to perform difficult tasks to a high standard, they will be trained in specific skills. Employee empowerment is invariably associated with business process re-engineering. Hammer and Champy called it the 'New World of Work' where jobs change from simple tasks to multi-dimensional work. This means that there would be job preparation changes from training to education, from following rules to exercising judgments, and managerial changes that involve changes from supervisors to coaches, including executive changes from score-keepers to leaders.

5. **Strategy** – Strategy is, ideally, organizational direction and scope over a long-term which mandates access of resources to meet the needs of its changing environment and in particular its markets, customers and employees so as to satisfy the expectations of its stake holders. Business process re-engineering drivers are strategic in nature. One can see that such factors as customers, competitions, costs, technologies, regulations, environments etc., are related to organization strategies. Strategy is well defined through vision,

mission, values and goals in consultation with the employees of an organization.

6. **Style** – Style is the philosophy, values and shared beliefs adopted by managers in their use of authority. Business process re-engineering style causes manager to change from supervisor to coach. Change incurred by process innovation is not only broad but deep, extending from the vision of managers to the attitudes and behaviors of the lowest level employee. Its significant behavioral component makes process innovation base change qualitatively different from other forms of large scale restructuring. Process innovation involves massive change not only in process flows and culture surrounding them, but also in organizational power and controls.

7. **Shared Values** – These are basic values and mission of the organization. They rise above profit target and growth objectively relating goals of the firm to deeper human needs and principles (Henlay-1991). In successful business process re-engineering operation, individual beliefs systems become aligned with the stated beliefs of the organization. Reengineering entails as great shift in the culture of an organization as in its structural configuration. Reengineering demands that employees deeply believe they work for their customers not for their bosses. Linked by common values there is an implication to their knitting, that individual must believe in self-management, self-development and skills upgradation.

Seven Principles of Reengineering

Hammer and Champy in their book "Reengineering The Corporations" suggested seven principles of reengineering to streamline the work processes and thereby achieve significant level of improvement in quality, delivery, speed, service and cost. Those principles are:

- Organize around outcome, not tasks.
- Identify all the processes in the organization and prioritize them in order of redesign urgency.

- Integrate information processing work into the real work that produces the information.
- Treat geographically dispersed resources as though they were centralized.
- Link parallel activities in the work flow instead of just integrating their results.
- Put decision point where work is performed and build control in the processes.
- Capture information once and at the source.

Three types of organizations generally go for business process re-engineering to improve their performance. They are:

- Organizations that are facing crisis.
- Organizations that foresee a crisis approaching. And
- Market leaders those want to get ahead of other organization.

Business process re-engineering is a management approach aiming at improvements by increasing efficiency and effectiveness of processes, in other words business process re-engineering is technique to help organizations fundamentally rethink how they do their work in order to dramatically improve customer service, cut operational costs, and become world-class competitors. It is basically the fundamental thinking and radical redesign, made to an organization's existing resources. It is more than just business improvising. It is an approach for redesigning the way work is done to better support the organization's mission and reduce costs. Leading organizations are becoming bolder in using this technology to support innovative business processes, rather than refining current ways of doing work.

How to Implement Business Process Re-Engeering

It is necessary to address approaches with the right thoughts so as to get acquired with the process easily. There are seven approaches to implement business process re-engineering:

- ❖ Start with mission statement that defines the purpose of the organization and describes we set apart from others in its sector or industry.
- ❖ Producing vision statements which define where the organization is going to provide a clear picture of the desired future position.
- ❖ Defining behaviors that will enable the organization to achieve its aims.
- ❖ Producing key performance measures to track progress.
- ❖ Relate efficiency improvements to the culture of the organization.
- ❖ Identifying initiatives that will improve performance.
- ❖ Build these into a clear business strategy thereby driving the project objectives.

Once these building blocks are in place the business process re-engineering exercise can begin.

Business process re-engineering goes beyond process changes. It impacts organizational structure, system, system options and management, front and back.

Business process re-engineering promises fundamental changes. It is therefore, of direct concern-personally, professionally and economically to all those working in that organization. A business process re-engineering means rethinking the way in which work is done. Clearly those who do that work have the right and expectation to be consulted, informed and involved in that change. After all change requires participation of people who must themselves change for organizational transformation to succeed. Proceeding as if those who do an organization's work are either not well enough informed or too deeply entrenched to contribute to change will result invariably in failure.

In essence, "reengineering is a particular way of using our minds, our businesses and anyone can learn it. It is a way of radical experimentalism of invention and reinvention. Constantly checked by the realities of the bottom line. To implement business process re-engineering, it is not enough for a leader to have vision, men and women who can commit themselves to the new ideal and of customer focus. But if the mobilization process to succeed, those followers must become leaders to finding their own sense of purpose in the shared challenge and spreading the call and vision of change" (J. Champy, Engineering Management, 1995). An organization, leaders, all sharing the same vision and purpose, can be a powerful force. But for that new organization to work, everyone in it must be given real work to do, work that focuses on making the vision and purpose real – in short, that focuses on reengineering.

"Mobilization begins at the top, with a vision and a business idea, but the energy comes from pushing authority and accountability down to where the action is."

– J. Champy

"Everything we have learnt about reengineering drives toward one solid conclusion: The rules of governance and self-governance for effective business enterprises today are being determined by their culture, not their organizational structure."

– (J. Champy)

Cultural value instructs our feelings so that we don't always have to pause and think before we act on them.

Chapter 12

ORGANIZATIONS OF FUTURE

Chapter 12
ORGANIZATIONS OF FUTURE

For organization to survive and strive in today's competitive environment, will need to change quickly and successfully. Managing change is now a core competence and can no longer be considered a discretion that professes the obsolete simple one-liner "nice to have." No organization can escape from a daunting array of challenges but force by new economy of today:

- ❖ In a world where no organization is protected from intense, unpredictable, disruptive, competition. (Hence, it is the 'organization' to make innovation everybody's job everyday)
- ❖ In a world where knowledge itself is becoming commodity, how do you cultivate an environment that engages and unleashes the gifts of each person's imagination, initiative and passion?
- ❖ In a world increasingly limited resources, how do we rethink what it means to win so that profit comes not from gaming the system but from changing the game for everyone?

Reinventing the technology and human accomplishment, one can't tackle these maga challenges if you are not willing to do three things: aim high; challenge the status and explore the opportunities for positive change. The organization of future will require a new mind-set. And fortunately, we are gradually getting familiar with post-modernist approaches to organizational competitiveness such as: Total Quality Management (TQM), Six-Sigma, lead production, lean organization, empowerment, team work and the like. For all post-modernist approaches three main themes are at the centre of change cycle: Empowerment, flexibility, and decentralization. The main message is the changing values of organizational members. Secondly, the focus shifts from organizational members to the need to develop new type of organizational leadership to enable achievement of the new ideas of people management. The most valuable message is that all organizational members to be self-aware and to develop reflective abilities; the necessity of changing our mental model of what constitute a successful organization. It is true that, the organization of future will empower every single employee to be the leader, decision maker and innovator. Extra-ordinary outcomes for work shall be achieved through extra-ordinary contribution by employees. This notion will be consistent with the slogan "Excellence in work is everybody's job… What people can contribute and what a high performing organization relies upon is a high degree of commitment, creativity, knowledge and skill. The conditions that gave rise to a high performing work organization are numerous and inter-dependent. The greater the number of these elements that are developed within an organization, the greater the performance pay-offs."

STRATEGIC IMPERATIVES FOR HIGH PERFORMANCE ORGANIZATIONS

❖ Workforce commitment is vitally important in achieving organizational goals and business objectives. And in order to execute strategies and achieve performance, profitability, the organization must have alignment and engagement of its workforce. Systems and processes must be in place to support employee engagement and commitment and it must be connected with motivation factors.

❖ In the organization of future, the success of organization depends on human resource management. Individuals will need to demonstrate foresight in navigating a rapidly shifting landscape of organizational forms, designs, and skill requirements. They will increasingly be called upon to continually reassess the skills they need quickly put together the right resources to develop and update those. Employees in the future will need to be adaptable life-long learner. The conscious organization is one that continually will examine in itself the commitment to become as aware as possible. It will have the collective will of vigilance, the collective commitment to continue development and collective courage to act.

❖ Organization must also be alert to the changing environment and adopt their workforce planning and development strategies to ensure alignment with future skills requirements. Ability to ensure organization's talent and continuously renewal of skills necessary for sustainability of business goals. A workforce strategy for sustaining business goals should be one of the most critical outcomes of human relation professionals should involve collaborating with future work skills.

❖ As the importance of people to the bottom line grows the rules for managing people are dramatically changing. Demographic, economic, technological and socio-political phenomena are driving the most drastic workforce changes, creating a workforce that is more diverse, mobile, informed, and in demand than ever before.

❖ Alarmingly, most organizations are not prepared to manage new generation talent. In fact research suggests that most large organizations are currently underutilizing their managerial and professional talent, are failing to understand the kind of support knowledge employee need to perform at their best, and are continuing to use industrial – age people management practices despite receiving less than optimal result.

❖ With knowledge and technology as the new economic currency, the majority of new jobs being created, require high skill levels and substantial knowledge expertise and the fast pace of change requires that skill and knowledge levels be continually upgraded.

❖ Across the world and across industries, employees are being freed from their desks and relieved of their traditional nine-to-five duty schedule. Growing use of wireless phones, high speed broad band connections and personal digital assists (DPAs) combined with rising proportion of work products that can be transmitted electronically, is completely redefining the concepts of workplace and workday.

❖ The rigid and reactive man-management practices of the past will be grossly insufficient for tackling the challenges of new age economy. Going forward, organizations will need to abandon these old practices for more flexible, anticipatory and democratic workplace practices.

These viewpoints provide the roots for thinking as to how to develop organizations of the future. As industry grows and changes are witnessed as regards how to produce quality products through better performances and employee satisfaction, one must focus on the changing concepts of people management and their performances at work. The environment drives the strategic architecture of the enterprise, either through anticipation of or reaction to major changes in economy. The organization's capacity to understand its environment and to make the kinds of strategic changes at the appropriate point in the change cycle will determines organization future. Effective organizations translate strategic imperatives into new organizational architectures and new leadership priorities. Lastly the relationship between strategy and organization design is critical. How an organization is organized will influence its focus and time horizons either encouraging or restricting its people's ability to develop creative strategies. The key to effective organization design requires an appreciation of the underlying duality of this challenge. How do we group people, processes and operating units in way appropriate to their unique competitive environments and strategic requirements and how we encourage divergence and cohesion, these are the critical areas to be examined while reshaping the organization design.

CHANGING PROFILE OF WORKFORCE

The management of 21st century is focused on contemporary issues such as human needs, global awareness, ethical behavior and team synergy. All these issues require a keen sense of behavioral sciences theories and applications that are foundations of new people management.

Talent and skills of the workforce is crucial factor for high performing organization. If businesses are to become high-performance organization, they must have employees who possess the right skills, abilities and mindsets. When sufficiently numbers of appropriately skill employees can't be found or trained organizational performance is undeniably crucial. Hewitt associates (study of US companies 2006) concluded that these organizations identified and developed skill employees consistently achieved high rates of share holders' return. Keeping skilled employees is considered as an important driver of firms financial performance is also observed by Accenture Woods. The institute for corporate productivity (US) found that among the most important drivers of people management are the need to execute strategies, stay competitive in the market place, serve customer well, and drive innovation – all elements in high performance.

❖ Now more than ever, it is imperative that organizations manage people well. In today, knowledge economy people knowledge, skills and relationships are an organization's biggest asset and main source of competitive advantage.

❖ Traditional geographic surroundings of the workforce are fast crumbling. In their place, a truly global job market is being built which was never seen before in industrial history and this has resulted in an increasing momentum of the employees' mobility and migration. Free-market reforms and technological advancements are creating a global labour market. No longer do employees need to limit their marketing skills solely within one country or region as they can now market themselves to organizations based anywhere in the world.

❖ The meaning of being 'at work' place is being completely redefined as employees across the globe connect via the latest communications technologies. A virtual workplace is taking hold today. Growing use of wireless phone, high-speed, broad-band connections made it possible to employees working in hotel rooms, at home and even on vacation. Across the world and across industries, employees are being freed from four to five office timing. Now they can very well operate from their home.

❖ Today workforce is getting more gender balanced. Significantly large numbers of women have entered the workforce. Women now represent 40% of the global workforce while more women enter the workforce, growing numbers of women are entering occupations previously reserved for the opposite gender. Today, women participate in all industries, profession and job levels.

❖ An autonomous and empowered workforce is taking driver's seat in controlling the direction and substance of professional lives. Technological and economic forces are giving them the capacity for greater authority on the job. Employees have the capacity and desire to be more influential on the job.

❖ Recent trends toward knowledge work and technology based communications are giving workers the expertise and skills to make more decisions about how they do their work. Knowledge workers have jobs or profession specific expertise that is not possessed by management making them logical decision makers in many areas. Via the internet's, employees have access to competitive intelligence business trends information and experts increasing their decision-making capabilities.

❖ While the knowledge economy is producing the employees with the expertise to make more decisions on the job, trend toward self-agency and free agency are giving employees the skills and desire to make these decisions. As organizations encourage employees to take more responsibility for their carrier development and employee benefits; they are creating a class of self-agents – employees with skills and desire to be self-sufficient on the job.

Taken together, the increased global, highly virtual, vastly diverse, autonomous and empowered workforces are so radically different from what employers have known in recent times that it will require them to entirely rethink their approach to managing people.

CHANGING PROFILE OF THE ORGANIZATION

The globalization exercises a direct effect on organizational performance is now acknowledged by organizations leaders. The ability to capture greater share of the market and remaining competitive are the vital drivers of their organizations and financial performance. Growth and quality improvement opportunities are the basic challenges put forth by globalization of business. More so mechanisms for transforming such factors like company structure, staffing, style, skills shared values, communication, capabilities and many more are the further challenges to be faced by the organizations. Kalpan and Norton (2006) noted that today organizations are challenged by the fact that intangible assets, such as knowledge, employees and research and development are playing an increasing role in corporate success and by the fact that globalization has dispersed those assets worldwide. These factors are driving companies to get better at alignment both physical and intellectual resources, internally and externally around the world. Therefore agility and resilience are likely to be characteristics of organizations that sustain performance over long period of time. The agility to absorb, react to, and even reinvent who you are as a consequence of change and agility is the ability to move quickly, decisively and effectively in anticipating and capability to manage change. Organizations with high adaptive capacities will drive their teams to perform better and better in the future. The other factors influencing organizational change are technology, political and regulatory changes, in people management. Organizations with well developed values, beliefs systems will perform better if those values are inculcated into the sense of purpose employees bring to their work. To deliver effective performance, organization needs to work hard to create a shared vision and values among their people.

THE CHANGE EFFECT

The changing profiles of workforce and organization will greatly magnify the change at workplace in the years to come. As next-generation workforce takes hold, it will render people management practices grossly insufficient and often determental to the bottom line. Past practices designed for dependent workforce will no longer sustain organizations.

The new workforce will be smaller and sufficiently skilled. It will be increasingly global, highly virtual and vastly diverse. Autonomous and Empowered. It will demand a new generation people management. Going forward organizations will need to abandon these practices for more flexible, anticipatory people management strategies.

Out of the next-generation workforce, a radically transformed leadership model is emerging. To get the most form workforce that is globally diverse, virtually connected and prepared to be authoritative on the job, organizations will distribute leadership responsibilities throughout the organization and transitional traditional leaders from commanding to influencing. Deciding what to do and how to do it will be responsibility of average employee, as opposed to the sole privilege of managers. Employees will take the decisions that are best made by them given their expertise and closeness to the issues at hand. Decentralized decision making shall be the case of organization's operations and democratic decisions making will aid organizations in unifying diverse workforces behind common goals.

With the advent of distributed leadership the role of traditional leader will dramatically shift. They will stop commanding and start influencing. They will promote a common organizational mission, using their passion for the business to excite employees. And they will work to ensure that employees will understand how they can contribute to the organizational mission.

Another key role for managers will be ensuring that the information system and knowledge sharing system are in place. With these systems, they will make available to the entire organization, information that was once reserved for executives and managers.

Organizations will minimize self-interest, employee differences and distance, build an organization, fabric and work to make participation in these cultures more silent than membership in any democratic, geographic and departmental sub-groups. Organizations will promote collectivist values. They will highlight the goals, standards and destinies that all employees shared and emphasis the commonalities among them; organizations will build cultures free of any discrimination, including that based on gender, age, and employment type and job location.

Organizations that are ignoring or procrastinating of these issues will almost certainly at first slowly and then with experimental speed face severe manpower crisis. Today's organizations need to heed the warning. They need to build upon new bright sparks of action relayed throughout this chapter and begin to proactively usher in the new people management. (Ref – Next Generation Talent Management – E Tucker and others – Hewitt.com/hr)

CHARACTERISTICS OF HIGH PERFORMANCE ORGANIZATION

While reviewing the literature of democratic, empowering in high performance organizations, there is considerable history behind the notions of high performance organizations. From their successful businesses and practices, experts have derived various principles for high performances in organizations from such literature as the American Management Association (AMA) and the Institute for Corporate Productivity (ICP). Surveys conducted in these High Performance Organizations (HPO) have delineated five major characteristics of such organizations:

1. **Their Strategic Approach** – The strategic approach of these organizations helped to determine their successes. The consistencies of these organizations can be measured to see how well these organizations 'walk the talk'. High performance organizations tend to establish clear visions that are supported by flexible and achievable strategic plans. They also have clearly articulated philosophies that set the standards for everyone's behaviour. In addition, they have leaders, managers and employees who behave consistently within the strategic plans and the company's philosophy.

2. **Their customer approach** – High performance organizations tend to have clear approaches to obtaining new customers, treating current customers and retaining customers. They also build the necessary infrastructure and processes to support their customer approach.

3. **Their Leadership Approach** – This describes the organization's strategy in managing people to achieve a particular set of behaviours. High Performance Organizations makes it clear about what behaviours employees must exhibit to execute the goals and departmental strategies of their organizations. Executives and managers set clear goals, understand their employees' abilities and guide their performances accordingly.

4. **Their Processes And Structure Approach** – This captures how organizations arrange their work processes, policies and procedures to support and execute strategy. High Performance Organizations have processes that reinforce strategy, setting up work flows and tasks that most effectively enable employees to meet internal and external customer needs within the limit of the strategy. Such companies tend to use a wide variety of metries to gauge the work for each department and the organization as a whole.

5. **Their Values And Beliefs Approach** – These are essential to helping company to execute its strategy and achieve its mission. High Performance Organizations typically have a set of well established values that are the deep drivers of employee behavior and are well understood by the vast majority of the employees. The values and beliefs are embedded in the organization and are constituent with the company's approach to leadership.

These five characteristics are the major drivers that influence organizational performance. Each interact with and influences the others creating a whole system. A change to one creates changes in others. Subsequently, the system tends to be in continual flux.

However, the future of business is impossible to foresee, too many uncertainties remain. For less mysterious, however, is the future of the workforce. As outlined in the previous chapter changing profile of employees a number of forces have set in motion a radical transformation of the workforce.

Organizational and people management transformation process implies massive changes in its literal meaning from one physical form to a unique different one. When we talk about people being transformed we mean that some of all of their behavior, appearance, acts of doing and managing things and culture, character, attitudes and relationships have undergone a rather complete change from the organizations their systems, beliefs, values and assumptions. Organizational renewals may suggest more gradual processes which are indeed when aiming for alternatives and revolutions. High Performing Organizations have gone through these revolutionary changes and have witnessed the positive effects of new people management. Such High Performing Organizations are successful because:

- They are recognized as leaders of at least some part of their industries and in a workforce context.
- Their people feel they have significant control over their own lives.
- Employees feel they are respected for their contribution they make.
- They feel they are contributing to something worth doing.
- They are more profitable than their competitors.

VALUES AND BELIEFS OF BEST RUN COMPANIES

Effectively managed companies have a 'sense of community' which is vividly expressed from their effective and optimal practices, values and beliefs:

- They interact frequently within at least one cohesive group in the company.
- They feel included and work hard at making others feel included.
- They like what they are doing and they like each other.
- They participate in setting goals, solving problems in organizational direction.
- They value individuality, creativity and differences of opinions.
- They are all pursuing the same general objectives.

- They believe in strong service to their customers and other stake holders.
- They maintain high standard of achievement.
- They hold each other mutually responsible, accountable for effective contribution.
- They feel fairly rewarded and recognized.
- They trust one another to be cognizant and supportive of their individual interests.
- They act ethically and with integrity in their relationship.
- They see themselves in others and others in themselves. They are empathic listeners and observers. They are attentive to each other's emotional needs.
- They assume responsibility for effective leadership and effective group processes.
- They work hard at inter-group with cooperation and team work.
- They reinforce culture with much listening, recognition, expressions of appreciation, humur, ceremony and tradition.
- They all have a sense of purpose that includes and transcends the job and the organization.

These conditions, in total may seem utopian to other organizations, but believe they are attainable in all kinds of organization, whether small, medium or large, whether it is manufacturing or service oriented organization. These are the underlying values of best managed companies.

ATTRIBUTES OF BEST RUN ORGANIZATIONS

Top Peter and R. Waterman based their study on 62 (diversified interests) organizations in their book "Passion for Excellence" and summarized eight attributes of empowered, excellent and innovative companies. These are the companies where they put empowerment into practice. These companies pay attention to four things; customer, innovation, people and leadership. The challenge for leadership is to empower employees so that they create greater innovations. Involve everyone in everything, use self managing teams, listen, celebrate, recognize, train and retain.' Eliminate bureaucratic rules and humiliating condition. This advice is powerful; practical to achieve productivity through people are some of the findings from this study. Empowerment to employees is an important ingredient in these high performing organizations. Secondly, 'open-book management' concept conceived by Jack stack, CEO, Springfield Remanufacturing Co, America pushes the ideas of empowerment to the extreme, usually with excellent financial results. The approach encourages every employee of the company to think like an owner to the business and then start to act like one. He further say to empower is to give someone power, which is done by giving individuals the authority to make decision, to contribute their ideas, to exert influence and to be responsible for participation, is an especially effective form of empowerment. Participation enhances empowerment and empowerment in turn enhances performance through people. The attributes of such organization are:

1. **Simple structure and lean staff** – They maintain a simple organization structure. They employ relatively few people. They do not prefer complex structures like matrix.

2. **Close to customer** – These companies pull all efforts to be close to customers and consider customer wishes as orders and delightment of customers as the ultimate goal.

3. **Productivity through people** – Employees are seen as key resources of the organization. This is emphasized through employee involvement programs as well as through activities that are designed to reinforce the belief that the employees' contributions to the successes of their organization are vitally important. They believe that organizational successes and personal successes of employees are same.

4. **Autonomy and Entrepreneurship** – Employees are given total control over their works and are encouraged to innovate in order to develop their products and services more competitively. The organization is broken down into meaningful units where each unit is given sufficient autonomy with proportionate responsibilities.

5. **Simultaneous loose and simultaneous tight emphases** – The basic ground rule applicable to all employees who adhered to them are given considerable freedom and their mistakes are tolerated.

6. **Stick to manageable** – These companies tend to stay neither small nor big and they stay close like well-knitted family. They do not fall into trap of becoming big diversified conglomerate company.

7. **A Bias for actions** – These companies are highly action-oriented and do not idle themselves in search of solutions. They do not engage in excessive analysis of a problem or allowing committees and other bureaucratic manifestation of a large organization to cause delays.

8. **Hands-on-value driven** – Senior executives lead the company by example. They promote a strong corporate-culture and continuously obtain feedback by keeping in close touch with core business activities.

Thus they create excellence in everything employees do.

PRACTICES OF BEST RUN COMPANIES (SELECTIVE)

What makes a company an

- Innovative Company.
- World Class Company
- Excellent Company
- TQM Company
- Empowered company.
- High performing company

They have the following attributes:-

- They are the best companies in all respect in their industrial world.
- They are growing faster & more profitable than their competitor.
- They hire & retain the best people.
- They respond quickly to changing market conditions.

- They are not satisfied with the status quo.
- They continually upgrade facilities, processes, skills, behavior & attitude.

THEIR PRACTICES

1. They empower their employees

Authority & information is given to employees to make wise business decision and to solve problems. When more people are empowered, the more they produce leaders who can set goals and define a (Milliken Co textile Manufacturer) vision of where the organization should go.

2. They are market driven

They understand and know what products and services their global customers want to buy. They focus their strategies on the customers goals & needs their priorities and thus become market driven with the goal of defect-free quality in everything they do. They create innovations in reducing cycle time, technology, delivery, support and service.

– (IBM Computers)

3. They see the world differently

They challenge traditional business thinking, status quo situation and accordingly go for to tailor the product to fit the needs of customer.

– (Proctor & Gamble Company)

4. They test new ideas

They think of implementing TQM in manufacturing and non-manufacturing areas, product strategies for product development and improvement, people strategies for HR development and service strategies to witness customer delite are their concern areas of quality improvement.

Their act of transplanting people ideas are considered more important than seeing if their ideas bore fruits. Zero defects, conformance to specifications, do it right the first time, the customer is always right seek perfection in every act of their doing.

– (AT & T)

5.   They make customer satisfaction an obsession

Putting quality service ahead of growth and an absolute dedication to quality & customer satisfaction are their main attributes. They believe that success is essentially the result of an unrelenting pursuit of customer satisfaction. For them customer satisfaction means quality. They believe that people, who work in an environment of respect, treat customer with respect. This positive environment is reflected in the company's relationship with its customer.

– (MBNA Credit Card Company.)

6.   They go for big dreams

They dream something bigger than what they do & getting employees to buy into the dream is considered important for business survival. Their employees training focuses on values, vision, mission and goals of company's business for comprehensive understanding of the dream. Commitment to excellent product/service that people take with them to work all the time, create quality beyond imagination.

– (Disney World Company.)

7.   They make quality part of their corporate values

They consider quality is not a program but a legacy, passed down to senior executives. Continuous improvement is a part of their culture. Reinforcing this quality culture is a major priority for them. They always remember that product/service is for our end user-customer. It is not for profit only. The profit automatically follows. Quality philosophy and specific measurement to safeguard the quality of all company products is highly inducted to each and every employees of the company.

– (Merck and Co.. Pharma. Co.)

8.   They do not compromise their quality standards

They just do not operate their business to make money. They always looked into and get involved in customer values, because these are critical to their success. Their philosophy of customer satisfaction is quality product, service, with good value to customer. That is their customer winning formula.

– (MC-Donald – Chain Restaurant Company.)

9.   They innovate on continuous basis

To improve upon quality of work life, quality of products and services, they create quality champions at every level. Kaizen – the never ending quest for perfection, potential development for H.R., pursuit for superior quality building, mutual trust, develop team performance, providing stable environment, collaborative problem solving, total quality management are some of the lessions they follow to create innovative environment in company.

– (NUMMI – Joint Venture Company of General Motors and Toyota.)

10. They have a vision and a strategy to make it happen

- Their vision is – a line of business must have number one in the industry.
- They believe strategy is not a lengthy action plan but rather the evolution or the central idea through continually changing circumstances.
- They believe quality is not a simple thing, but an aura, an atmosphere, an overpowering feeling that a company is doing everything with excellence, and that the customer is elevated,

enhanced in his self-worth and image bettered by his relationship with the company.

- "Their mission is, we want a company where people find a better way every day, of doing things; & where by shaping their own work experience, they make their lives better & your Company best."

– (General Electric Motor.)

11. Their process effectiveness

- Their outputs (products and services) exceed all customer expectation.
- Their work is defect free, zero defects.
- They are industry leader & earn more value than competitors.
- They are bench marked by others.

12. Their process efficiency

- Their processes are defect free, low cost, no wasted cycle line.
- There is no output variation, no rework.
- They established zero cost of poor quality (COPQ) and have high productivity and asset utilization.

With their built-in – characteristics, they achieved world class status in their ways of doing the business.

OPEN BOOK MANAGEMENT (OBM)

As per business English dictionary: open book management is a "management style that encourages employees to work for a company's success by sharing information with them about all its operations and results."

Open book management is the way of managing company demonstrably without concealment that motivates all employees to focus on helping the business grow profitably and increasing the return on the human capital, that will enable them to understand how the company makes money and how their action affect its success and bottom line. A crucial component of open book management is that employees have a direct stake in the company's success. The goal is to persuade every employee to think and act likes a owner in the business. As a result, employee's goals and actions can be more closely aligned with those of the owners, greatly reducing the agency problem between employee and owner. It is believed under this intervention that a company performs best when its people see themselves as partners in the business rather than as a hired hands. The technique is to give employees all relevant financial information about the company so they can make better decisions as employees. This information includes but not limited to revenue, profit, cost of goods, cash flow and expenses. Obviously, open book management, the approach focuses on shifting employee's attention beyond the parameters of their own jobs and towards overall performance of the business. The objective of open book management is to get employees think like owners of the company. This objective is reached by sharing information about the company direction and financial performance as well as sharing final rewards of the company's success with employees.

Open book management has two parts: sharing financial information (opening the books) of developing a process that enables employees to use business information to improve the management for this process, you have got to do five things:-

- Share information that is relevant to employee's day-to-day jobs.
- Build employees skills so they can understand the information.
- Create a common vision and shared business.
- Develop leader's skill and a process where employees can use their knowledge to improve the company.
- Design a reward system that reinforces making business improvements.

Under open book management process that develops overtime is:

- Hard work
- Sharing good and bad news.
- Group responsibilities for members.
- Sharing rewards and risks.
- Empowering people to make decisions.
- Treating employees like adults.
- Individual responsibilities.
- Having courage to do it.

Employees are business people company by sharing every relevant thing with employees help them figure out how to improve the business. Company can establish open book management to clear away their obstacles to improve performance. Following are the reasons why companies go far open book management.

- To become more competitive.
- To enhance customer serviced product quality
- To empower a team work or employee involvement efforts.
- To increase shareholders value.
- To reduce costs and increase profits.
- To build trust.
- To enhance internal communication efforts
- To focus employees' actions on business challenges.
- To create a company of winners.

Overall, open book management teaches employees how their company is in business to make money. Employees may work for a variety of reasons, what the company needs them to do is to help it make money. Getting employees into action and excitement of business and teaching them their role in helping their company make money is what open book management is all about. It suits to the companies that are interested in making more money and getting employees to act like business people. However, for the process to work, you have got to make the fundamentals fit your company's culture and business challenges. A company that wants to implement open book management, they believe in the following benefits:-

- Employees in the company can make a contribution to its performance.
- Employees deserve to share in the rewards they help create.
- Company can teach people what company knows about the business.
- Employees can learn about what makes business succeed.

The open book management concept developed by (Jack Stack, CEO, Spring Field Co.) argued that companies do better when employees care not just about quality, efficiency, or any other single performance variable, but about the something that managers are supposed to care about the success of the business. It spread the burden of profits and loss responsibility for the profit and loss account of business unit that is generally given as a reward to raising the managers, to everyone in the organization. With open book management, the idea is that everyone has a certain amount of profit and loss responsibility. As said by John case, open book management – the great game of business, is a process, a pattern, a system, a strategy, a way of thinking. If you want to fully leverage the power of open book management, you must persistently work the process. The following are the core characteristics or practices most exceptional companies are practicing. These core practices make up the process. They help shape the behavior of employees and the way of thinking that is critical to making this happen:-

- Begin with right leadership.
- Share the way before how.
- Open the book and teach the number.
- Apply high improvement planning.
- Focus on critical number.
- Act on right drivers.
- Provide a stake in the outcome.
- Keep score.
- Follow the action.
- Create an early win.

The principles of open book management are an effective way to help get everyone involved and share recognition of a problem or opportunity. The open book management approach gets other thinking about critical issues. The thing that keeps you awake at night can start keeping others awake as well. Open book management literally opens the books. Many companies share financial information, industry trends, quality reports, customer service rating and so forth. Too often the data that drives a business is accessible to only a few in organizations. So when leaders announce change, no one else see why it is necessary. Open book management changes that. Hence are some of the elements that can make open book management works:-

- Provide access to critical business information.
- What are the challenges facing your business.
- What are the opportunities?
- How are you doing financially?
- What do customers say?
- What are the measures do you use to make strategic decisions? Consider opening these up to everyone;
- All this information must be timely.
- Make sure people can interpret these data. It will do no good to give people financial information if they can't read a balance sheet.
- Provide whatever training is necessary.
- Give people a stake in the outcome, linking pay, bonus and incentive etc.
- Give them authority to act on when you give employee information they need to be able to do something with it.
- Make sure employees get data in a way they can believe. They must trust the source of the data. If they don't trust you, they won't trust the data.

Open book management works best when the entire organization focuses on these principles, but if you can use them within a single department, it won't be effective, but it will be far better than what most employees get in organization.

John case narrated some merits of open book management philosophy: Everyone sees and understands the financial and numbers critical to the firms performance.

- Employees learn that at least part of their job is to move those numbers in the right direction.
- Employees have a direct stake in the company success.

In conclusion, open book management means opening a company's financial statement to all employees and providing the education that enables them to understand how the firm makes money and how their actions affect the bottom line. It is a method of managing without concealment that involves all employees in focusing on how to grow the business profitability. Open book management is key to organizational democracy. A huge part of it is interactive education about how your business works, and enquiry into how to make it work even better. The basis of open book management is that the information received by employees should not only help them do their job effectively, but help them understand how the company is doing as a whole.

Though open book management seems to be a unconventional idea that firms are most effective if their accounts are left open for all the employees to see as and when they wish, at the same time as the employees are taught to understand better the full financial picture. Traditionally, only a handful of senior executives are made to feel responsible for whether a business makes money or not. Open book management attempts to extend this feeling of responsibility to everybody in the organization. As per Jack Stack, open book management encourages company owners to open up their books and expose their financial results to their employees in the belief that the employees will make better decisions and be more committed.

Chapter 13

INDUSTRIAL DEMOCRACY – A REVIEW

- ❖ What Is Industrial Democracy
- ❖ Industrial Democracy in India
- ❖ Industrial Democracy – A Myth or Reality

Chapter 13

INDUSTRIAL DEMOCRACY – A REVIEW

WHAT IS INDUSTRIAL DEMOCRACY? (ID)

"The milk of human kindness is less opt to turn sour if the vessel that holds it stands steady, cool and is not too often un corked"

— (Santayana)

"For democratic polity to exist it is necessary for a participatory society to exist. The most important area is the industry. If democracy is to be justified in governing the state, it must also be justified in governing economic enterprise."

— (D. H. Cole and others)

We used the term – Industrial Democracy to embrace all substantial shift of power from management to employees, from command to control to way of operating to a more democratic style and analyze its historical development to establish what industrial democracy we mean. Let us assume the participation in the policy and in industry have the common values and purposes of a) giving dignity to the participatory individuals; b) protecting their interests and the benefits to be derived from the application of these values to each domain could be complementary to; substitute for or interdependent of each other. The goals are complementary in the sense that increments of one are beneficial to the other. They reinforce each other in two senses: a) by learning the values and skills of participation in one domain a person is better prepared for effective participation in the other: b) the benefits derived from participation in one expertise are additive to the benefits derived from the other (Ref – From political to industrial democracy, Robert E. Lane, Yale university).

The term industrial democracy is treated here as an ultimate goal to strive for in the same way as we are striving to achieve a more democratic society. It is clear that employee's participation, involvement and empowerment in management decisions affecting their work may take a wide range of forms. There are direct forms of participation, where individual employees or group of employees are given an opportunity to influence the immediate working environment. There are indirect forms of participation and involvement in which employees are given the right to elect their representatives to various works committees, joint councils, joint consultations or employee election committees, Board of Management and Worker Directors, etc. Such representatives may have the opportunity to influence wider aspects of the work environment and to contribute to a greater or lesser extent in management policies. But, there are some major issues of different forms of participation:

- ❖ To what extent management is prepared to share power with employees and to develop responsibility and authority for decision making?
- ❖ What is the role of union in participation?
- ❖ How far equal opportunities for participation available to all employees?
- ❖ What benefits does participation have for employer and employees.

Employee participation is an important industrial relations issue, which may impact on different enterprises in different ways, economic, political, legal and social trends have affected the directions of developments in participation in India and overseas. For a more positive attitude toward the adoption of new technologies and modern management practices, consultation and involvement is advocated by management to allow employees maximum opportunities to influence the design of supporting systems. Decentralization and delegation of decision making responsibility are also identified as major areas contributing to workforce cooperation and effectiveness. Lastly, as a generalization the evidence shows that employees prefer forms of participation which give them greater skills through training and the provisions of more extensive information by management. There is also evidence to show that attitude to participation vary with age, seniority and level of skills and education. Overall, it appears that more skilled, better educated and more long serving employees are more favorably inclined toward forms of participation than younger, less skilled and uneducated employees.

To begin with I shall make it clear what I mean by industrial democracy. The term as used here refers primarily to participation by the employees who actually work in an enterprise. At present stage, development of industrial democracy, employees have the right to participate in managerial decisions. 1) It is, management that recognizes this right and provides employees with actual chances to take part. 2) Employees may participate in decision making processes at the top, middle levels as well as in the shop floor or at the bottom level of an enterprise. The nature of decisions in which employees participate, therefore, will be different at each level. 3) Employee participation should be put into operation as words; the degree of democratization of a group can be measured by the scope and depth to which its members are able to share in such decisions and their execution.

The term industrial democracy generally refers to the democratization of industrial relations between worker union and management. There is however, another aspect of industrial relations namely employer-employee relations. The ultimate goal of industrial democracy, in my opinion is to democratize fully the latter aspect of industrial relations in a given industry. The two aspects of industrial relations and employer, employee relations are in reality closely inter-connected. Factors determining one are often found inter-locked with those determining the other. Never the less, the forms of democracy in these two aspects are not necessarily alike, while democracy in employer-employee relations is primarily characterized by employee participation; union-management consists in the unions right and ability to negotiate management as an equal body. Where unions have right, they also able to affect managerial decisions and do restrict the arbitrariness of management. This effect which a union can have upon management may be called "participative." Since participation includes those actions that in some way or other affect the managerial decision making process. In this sense and in this sense alone, there is a similarity between these two forms of democracy in industrial relations.

Secondly the idea of industrial democracy may be the focus for emerging knowledge economy and the subsequent structural changes within big firms in the global economy. Given the rise of a new technological reality, more than ever before, many corporate bodies are forced to push for decentralized power structure in which their knowledge workers are encouraged to participate in organizational issues in a democratic order. In the post capitalist work place, the professional workforce requires little direct supervision from managers and more participation in decision making process. Furthermore, the discourse on industrial democracy enhances empowerment of employees in the light of fundamental changes within the structure of contemporary economy. The key to industrial democracy system is in decentralizing the organization into autonomous groups which are capable of doing manufacturing, marketing, R and D and people management. Facilitating a shift, the information based organization of the knowledge workers introduce innovation through an organized entrepreneurship and by implementing industrial democracy enhances an organization's readiness, willingness and ability to change (ackoff-1989). In this respect democratic organizational design makes it possible for the discipline of innovation to embrace the highest form of ethical-moral judgment: a democratic decision making process. Since in a democratic decision making the way a choice is made is critical, the design of an effective process of facilitating participation requires understanding of the systematic characteristics of an enterprise, put other way the idea of industrial democracy refutes the myth of entrepreneurial hero in favor of an organized entrepreneurship because the performance of an enterprise is never equal to the sum of the performance of its parts taken separately as it is product of their interactions.

Today, management of industry by employees organized to do the job is not a mere dream. It is the historic trend. It is the people toward which every forward move of employees have pointed, whether intended or not but it can't be achieved without deliberately planning it. Industrial democracy is freedom within a business frame work. It is a strategy for organizational design and a way leading and managing organization. It is achieved when an organization uses the principles of democracy to design the way it operates daily, thereby cultivating a work place that enhances employee potential, achieve its business goals and positively impact the community. It is well known that involving people in making decisions that affects them has a lot of benefits. It is a means of motivating employees, developing them and fostering ownership and commitment to a course of action. It is pretty obvious that employees are more likely to be motivated if they feel some ownership over plans and out comes rather than if they are simply told what to do, as if they were robots. However, the great idea to include employees in deciding how things should be done, when top management makes a strategic decision, there are of many ways of executing the strategy. In these cases employees are more likely to buy in to a specific implementation plan if they own it, if they have helped to develop it.

In conclusion, every new creation in history has evolved because we as human beings have been ready and attuned to replace old belief systems with new belief systems. Democratization of the work place requires that the people in the work place identify their visions, principles, values, goals and develop shared understandings as to how the democratic workplace can and should be organized. Therefore, a change in practice at work will first emerge when we are willing to change our belief system from our current reality to the desired reality. Numerous studies show that companies that empower their employees by allowing them to participate in the decision-making process can expect a variety of benefits. Along with a heightened sense of responsibility, employees report that they are committed and more motivated to causing a direct and positive impact on their performance and on the performance of their companies. Furthermore, the greater the degree of influence granted to employees the greater the results,

(228 | Pillars of Industrial Democracy) the more influence and an increase in the participation for performance management. Industrial democracy is about people. It is for managing people. It is about changing people in the way they think about organizing, inspiring, motivating, enabling, involving and empowering people for value-adding operational work. It is about managing our positive man-management itself.

Unfortunately, nothing is that simple. Industrial democracy prescribes committed actions not words, and difficult long term actions at that, not just one-shot expedients like reengineering management. Industrial democracy involves a long journey that will last years together as we have seen while reviewing history of employee participation in management. To be straight, industrial democracy requires a change in a company's whole culture, the way they are doing the things. We do work with people. How they work? What are their expectations, what are their traits must be known to us. Fortunately, for most of us 'Yes we can' yet is not a curse. It is an opportunity for us to rediscover ourselves. We must look into our culture, character, climate and commitment. We must find the resources we need to do our jobs by democratic way. Everybody, not just owners and managers, now believed in a great new secular faith of growth. And growth is not just economic but personal, social, cultural and spiritual as well. Business people began to see business world in a new way. They began to realize that intelligent people who care about their jobs will make the right decision when given right information and gradually, they offered to live with their employees decisions. This state of mind set started participating employees in management of their jobs and work places. The best thing is you let the people know that you understand their view-point but that all your business experience tells you that the things has to be done differently, then you stand aside. That is what all the talk about empowerment really comes down to, is not it? To help people rise to the level of maturity where they will make the right and reasonable decisions. We gradually started to abandon the management credo "get it right, then keep it going" and started embracing the credo "get it right and make it better and better and better." Democratic work places are part of the most successful companies today because they enable an innovative and collaborative environment.

Democratic governments throughout the world have at one time or other struggled with the best way to implement "a government of the people, by the people and for the people", so it should not be too surprising that there is a resistance to the concept within the corporate world. Industrial democracy is achieved when an organization uses the principles of democracy to design the way it operates daily, cultivating a workplace that enhances employee potential in achieving its business goals and thereby positively impacting the community. Industrial democracy is not about every one voting, but about everyone having a vote. It is not about employees always being able to decide what should be done – it is about including employees in decisions about how things should be done. When top management makes a strategic decision, there are often many different ways of executing the strategy. Employees who are close to a product, service or customer can provide invaluable inputs and information in terms of deciding how to implement a strategy. Employees are also more likely to buy into a specific implementation plan if they own it - in other words, if they have helped to develop it.

A democratic work place is not just a good idea but it does take a special kind of collective commitment to make it happen.

The study of industrial democracy attempts to recontextulize the study of empowerment in management by tracing the linkage between concepts of human relations, workers participation and involvement. Reforming the linkage between these concepts proceeds and analyzes the various interventions to show the often neglected complexity of this area of debate.

INDUSTRIAL DEMOCRACY IN INDIA

Over the last several years a combination of powerful social, cultural, political, economic and industrial pressures has created a worldwide demand for greater participation and democratization. Employee participation in management is only one of the manifestations of this global trend. Contemporary interest in promoting workers participation in large measure due to democratic or socialistic ideology desire to increase union power and belief that participation enhances productive efficiency, foster industrial harmony and enriches human personality (Derber-1970). Employee participation is no longer a question of "whether" but of "how." In India, formal representative participation has taken in the form of collective bargaining and works committee, shop council, joint council, joint consultation and management of industrial relations with the intervention of government. Secondly, the scheme of industrial democracy in India should be viewed not only as politico-legal doctrine but as an instrument of socio-economic change too. With this end we tried in brief to identify the concept of industrial democracy in India.

Industrialization and economic development in accord with uniform pattern everywhere throughout the world, much like the evolutionary development from the feudal to the capitalists and from capitalists to the socialist order of society. The fact, traditional practices are still in force, therefore, points to disreputable backwardness which is an obstacle to the democratization of Indian industries.

Industrialization in India basically a process initiated and promoted by the government rather than a movement which arose from among the people. Again the early leaders of industrialization came from feudal, capitalist classes, who were accustomed to the traditional value, orientations of feudal India. As a consequence managerial policies and industrial relations in India were from beginning and are even today tried with various pre-modern traits. It has been said that, for instance that the protestant ethic, the competitive and individualistic nature of social interaction and the rationalistic character of industrial organization contributed constructively to the industrial productivity and economic growth of western countries. In non-western countries including India, however, the same factors may not be useful. By contrast, from the view point of western industrialism, the nationalistic motivation of entrepreneurs, the immobility of workforce, personal loyalty to employers and paternalistic care for the welfare of employees may seem to be insufficient and feudalistic. Never the less, in terms of specific and Indian social and cultural background there factors did not foster industrial progress and did not raise the standard of labor.

The rapid transformations that have been taking place in India from post-independence period and particularly since last three decades are really logical and appreciative and conducive for establishment of industrial democracy at workplace. These transformations are roughly in a direction that can be called democratic and on values as well as practical ground must not be denied particularly, in the decades 1990–2000 and 2000–2010, due to liberalization, privatization and globalization (LPG), industrial cultural changes are very fast and to some extent positive. The factors that have brought about these trends change include

a. post-independence labor legislations aimed at protecting the interest of employees an represented by trade union and labor laws
b. A rapid spread of unionization of industries
c. The introduction of various technological innovation, such as automation
d. Changes in attitudes of industrial workers specially of those young generation toward work and authority in industry. Attitudes which have been influenced by the new educational system and by the democratic social atmosphere of post-independent India,
e. The effect of recent rapid economic growth which has brought about an expansion of business, a shortage of highly skilled employees, increased employee mobility and a general improvement of the national standard of living. And lastly,
f. The latest processes of globalization of industrial world.

Now there is a governing tendency for Indian management to attach importance to employees who actively exert their individual talents rather than maintaining the traditional attitude of passive obedience. Apart from public the public sector, some progressive organizations like Tata, Birla, Godrej, Infosys, Wipro, Uniliver, TVS and Maruti, among others, have come to realize the significance of encouraging employees' participation and involvement in managerial decisions. If the managerial policies of Indian industries are to be modified and if they are to shake-off the autocratic-paternalistic patterns with speed then purposeful efforts must be made to this end by the government. Likewise if the management, (232 | Pillars of Industrial Democracy) in this era of technological innovation and generally of democratic trends, really want to keep up the morale and motivation of its employees and to maintain high standards of work productivity, it must somehow reform its practices in a new and more democratic direction. Employees will of course have to be fitted into such reformed practices but it is the managers who must devise them or allow for their development and thereby create an environment in which they will be viable. The management's innovative role here, as in other aspects of business, is crucial. Therefore, and most important, employees should be given ample opportunities and adequate encouragement to participate in management decisions. This is the logical outcome of the treatment of employees as partners. Democratization of industrial management is an urgent necessity in Indian industries because there are nascent, but inevitable, trends toward democracy within and outside the enterprise. Democratization of workplace can alone meet the needs of the times.

INDUSTRIAL DEMOCRACY – A MYTH OR REALITY

"In the age of hand-crafting, the dominant forms of organization were that all-powerful kingdoms and religious institutions and hand-craft men guilds. Just as the age of machine-crafting led the emergence of today's organization, ending the dominance of guilds, kingdoms and religious institutions like churches etc, so too will the age of mind-crafting give rise to new, more chaordic concepts of organization that will end the dominance of today's organizational structure."

– (Dee Hock.CEO and Founder of VISA)

Greater transparency is an unstoppable force. The internet e-mail make it far easier for firm to supply information and harder for them to keep business secrets. With greater transparency will come greater accountability and better corporate behavior. Rather than engage in futile resistance to it, firms should actively embrace transparency and rethink their values and generally get in better shape.

– (Den TapScott-Co-Author of The Naked Corporation)

Democratic practices, therefore, are central to any of the organizations because it involves and empowers employees to run amazing and profitable organizations as we are seeing throughout the world. In the organizations of today and of future, it will be much more important to have a clear sense of purpose and sound principles which are well supported by value systems with firm commitments. As discussed earlier, we have focused on problems and solutions. Various interventions/solutions already exist and are being put into practice by successful business houses at this very moment. What has yet to be developed is a cohesive system that incorporates many of these concepts/solutions clearly through a defined set of "laws" from which to govern by. Furthermore, once this cohesive structure has been established, it will require new tools to allow functioning. This will mean new tools to facilitate the participation of countless inter-connected yet decentralized individuals and systems for tracking the employees' contribution. This will also include tools to improve collaborative efforts and problem solving measures as well as transparency and feed-back mechanisms.

Perhaps the most relevant question is how easily can a particular type of organization implement these interventions/solutions and participation, involvement and empowerment (PIE) concepts? Pioneers reap the greatest rewards. And as the next few years unfold regardless of the type of organization seeking to become an enterprise of success and full of excellence. You will have to chance to participate in the great reconceptualization of work that is taking place right now.

There have been and still exist many myths about industrial democracy. I believe the glass-ceiling at the work place was a reality until the 20th century, but with the advent of the 21st century the ceiling has become a myth and rightly so. The fierce, competitive environment currently existing throughout the globe is forcing many organizations to transform themselves to a new paradigm for manufacturing; customer service and satisfaction-internal as well as external, quality management etc. organizations are being forced to implement modern management practices like Total Quality Management (TQM), Business Process Engineering (BPR), Management Re-Engineering (MR), Organization Restructuring (OR), Work Improvement Teams (Quality Circles, Kaizen, just-in-time etc) ultimately aim to improve their operations, services and quality of products and quality of work life, so that they can serve their customers better than their competitors. In general, it means that organizations having long-term commitments and ongoing improvements for overall organizational quality and its systems with all employees at all levels and in all work processes. This causes the employees to actively participate with each one in order to contribute in making the organization healthy. Democratic work place culture is taking shape in India and it is more visible in the private sector than in the public sector and these organizations are witnessing positive mind-set changes on the part of the managed and managers. They are also reaping the fruits of collaborative management. It amply proves that industrial democracy in India is not a myth but reality.

BIBLIOGRAPHY

Author	Book Title	Publisher
Dr. Rajendra Sen	Employee participation in India	ILO Publication – 2012
M. Musta O. Sharma	Workers participation in management	Deep and Deep Publication, Delhi – 1998
Lewin Davin and others	Participation in Organization	Oxford books online, Magazine 2010
Jan Kees, N. Torka	Understanding workers participation and Organizational performance	Emerald Group Publishing Ltd. – 2011
Juliett Summers and Jeff Hyman	Employee participation and Company Performance	Joseph Rowntree Foundation
Allien and others	Employee participation and Involvement	Jim Corway Foundation, 1997
M.C. Arole	Industrial Participation	Pitman Press, London – 1979
Bradley K. and Gelb A.	Cooperation at work- The Mondragon Experience	Heinemann, London – 1983

Author	Book Title	Publisher
	Participation in change and Role of employee Involvement	European Foundation, Dublin-1990
Heller F. and others	Organizational Participation – Myth and Realities	Oxford University Press, London, 1998.
Penvacel J.	Workers Participation	Sage Publication, New-York – 2001
Dr. G. Ratnakar	Workers Participation in Management	KITS Warangal (AP)-2012
P Y Lee	Workers Participation in Management – Myth and Reality	N V Publication, New Delhi-1945
P Venkat Raman	Workers Participation in Management	APH Publishing New Delhi – 2007
Alexcander K.C.	Participatory Management	Shriram Centre For Industrial Relations, New Delhi – 1973
Clegg N.A.	Trade Unionism and Collective Bargaining	Oxford Basil Blackwell, 1996.
Agrawal R.D.	Political Dimension of Trade Union	Tata MC Graw Hill, New Delhi – 1972
-	Gandhian Economic Philosophy	Vora and Company, Mumbai – 1963
R. Russel and V. Rus(edi)	International Handbook of Participation in Organization	Oxford University Press, Vol II – 1991
Hartley I.F.	Employment Relations	Blackwell, London – 1992
	The Future of Employee Representation	British Jr. of Industrial Relations Vol-35, 1997
Keep E. and Rainbird N.	Industrial Relations – Theory and Practice	Oxford, Blackwell – 2003

Author	Book Title	Publisher
Knell J.	Partnership at Work	DT1, London – 1994
Knell J.	The Mutual Gain Enterprise	Harvard Business School press, 1994.
Levine D.I.	Reinventing The Work Place – How Business & Employee can both win	D.C. Brooking Institution, Washington, 1995
Scarborougbh	The Management of Enterprise	Basing Stroke Macmillian, 1996
Thomson P. & Warthurstc	Workplace of Future	Basing Stroke Macmillian, 1998
Walton R.E.	From Control To Commitment in Workplace	Cambridge H. B. Review books, 1995
Das N.G.	Industrial Democracy in India	Asian Publication House, Mumbai – 1962
Gadre Kamla	The Coming Struggle of Trusteeship	Tranship Foundation, New Delhi
Jean Dreze	India's economic Development & Social Opportunity	Oxford University press, New Delhi – 1995
Kennedy V.D.	Union Employee And Government	Menaklal, Mumbai 1966
Kohli A.S. & Sharma S. k.	Labor Walfare And Social Security	Anmol Publications Pvt. Ltd., New Delhi – 1977
Lambart R.D.	Workers, Factories, And Social Change	Printiceton University press, New Delhi – 1963
Mamoria C.B.	Dynamics of Industrial Relations	Himalaya Publication House, Allahabad – 1969
Pertman Selig	A Theory of Labor Movement	MacMillian & Co., New York, 1928
Hyman J.	Managing Employee Involvement	Sage Publication, London

Author	Book Title	Publisher
Patter Field	The Business of Employee Empowerment	Quorum Books, Westport – 1999
Lawler E.E.	High Involvement Management	Jossey – Bass, San Francisco
Turner L.	Democracy at Work	Corniwell University Press, Ithaca, 1991
Vroom V.H.	Work And Motivation	Thomson Press
Thomas A Patter Field	The Business of Empowerment	Green Hood Publishing group, 1999
Kelly G.A.	The Psychology of Personal Contracts	W. W. Nortton, New York – 1980
CharanRam & others	The Leadership Pipeline	San Francisco, Jossey-Bass, 2001
Kravetz	The Human Resource Revolution	San Fraansisco, Jossey-Bass, 1988
Drucker Peter	Managing in a Time of Great Change	Plume Books, New York 1998
Schurz W.	The Human Element, Productivity, Self Esteem & The Bottom Line	Jossey – Bass, San Francisco – 1994
Dale B.G. & others	A Guide to Continueous Improvement	Blackwell Oxford, 1992
David Croton	Employee Engagement	P & M – 2010
Hollish Head. & others	Employee Relations	F.T. Pitman Publishers, G.B., 1999
	Human Relations at Work	Mc-Grew Hill Publications, New York – 1996
Schleh E.C	Management by Results	Mc-Grew Hill Publications, New York – 1961
Dr. Katkhede V.R.	Transform to Perform Total Performance Management	Himalaya Publication House, Mumbai – 2011

Author	Book Title	Publisher
Dr. Katkhede V.R.	Employee Development – A Gateway to Organization Success	Himalaya Publication House, Mumbai- 2012
	Talent Management – Acquisition, Retention and Development	Himalaya Publication House, Mumbai – 1972
Waltson E. Richard	From control to Commitment	HBR Mar-Apl – 1985
Mayer & Allen	Commitment to Workplace	Sage Publication, London
Dr. Katkhede V.R.	Human Relations in an Industry	U. N. Published Ph.D. Thesis. Marathwada University, Aurangabad – 1977